# SNAPSHOTS

# SNAPSHOTS

# BY

# GIBRAN TARIQ

SNAPSHOTS

## ACKNOWLEDGEMENTS

This book, written in 1997, has taken this long to get to print but I pray that the sentiments expressed herein are still timely and inspiring. All praises are due to Allah.

I thank my family, my friends, and those who will enjoy this work.

*January 1ˢᵗ*

*Don't believe the hype! There are only 7 days a year. Monday, Tuesday, Wednesday, Thursday, Friday, Saturday, Sunday. It's just that they come at U 358 more times in a bewildering array of brilliant disguises.*

-Ali-

Until you have made a happy landing at that place called **YOU**, there is no need to even consider making resolutions. You don't know who you are, so how can you choose wisely? Without intimate knowledge of your real needs, you will tend to choose what speaks loudest or sparkles brightest. There must exist a continuing sense of loyalty to yourself, and then you must crush all the remnants of the person you were molded to be by others. Then you work with what's left. That's the framework that leads to **YOU**. HAPPY LANDING!

## January 2nd

*Anything is something when you have nothing on*
*your mind*
-Ali-

Be Real! When you begin to take meaningful steps to throw off the shackles of oppression that yoke you spiritually, physically, mentally, financially, you must accept the fact that affirmations, no matter how potentially powerful, do not work unless you are on a level playing field. Be real about that fact. Too many people start the year under the false illusion that affirmations are some sort of "poetic" genies and that if they shout them loud enough or often enough, seeming magic will occur. Not hardly. Be real. An affirmation concedes nothing without the dirty work that must precede it.

## January 3

*Life is a point between birth and death where*
*nuthin' exists beyond good and evil except*
*The miserable failure of men who throw themselves*
*in open competition with God.*

-ali-

Consider this: one reason for the low self-esteem of many black women is that they willingly participate in the condescending ritual of allowing the black man to set himself up as a rival to God. In the name of love, they silently watch as their existence is slowly diminished while emotional murder is perpetuated upon them. God, in His Infinite Wisdom, created woman to be a queen, a mother, a nurturer, but merely because man, in his puny arrogance, feels he can make better use of her as a "ho" or a dope fiend, she permits herself to be transformed. Why? Because of the foolish desire to love someone not her equal!

.

## January 4

*A lie is the handicapped orphan of man's crippling inability to understand the power of truth.*     *–Ali–*

All things considered, a man elevates or reduces those he love according to his own stature, so the law of correspondence dictates that if he seeks to reduce you, you are greater than he is. If he must cut you down to size in order to harness your gigantic potential, then he is truly not deserving of you to begin with. And who are you to let him tamper with what God has created? O, black woman, is it any wonder that your self esteem is low? You are a deposed queen who left her throne to wallow in the mud.

## January 5

*On every journey, there are milestones along the way that indicate to the weary traveler just how far he has come. These milestones are not laurels upon which to rest your tired soul. Instead, they must push you forward toward greater progress.   —Ali-*

There are no vacation stops on the road to self-improvement. Once you set sail on the journey to the new "YOU", there are no layovers, no pit-stops, no shade tree celebrations... It is a constant, continuous getting-there. All gains must be unified and solidified until their development is as consistent and reliable as a favorite recipe. This means that the results are precisely the same each time they are employed. Lacking this consistency means you're still only experimenting which in turns means that you're squandering your energy. Don't indulge in such waste. The key is to provide only the necessary amount of cure to a problem to heal it. Anything more may aggravate the wound.

## January 6

*Knowing when to celebrate a victory rests upon your ability to recognize if you have actually broken through or if your enemies are merely resting. –Ali-*

No consolation prize exists for coming in second in the race to fulfill yourself. Coming close means you failed. You have decided to embark upon the journey. Now, you will be compelled to pull yourself up by your own bootstraps. At no time will the toil be easy. Rather, the task will be as unpopular as producing bricks without straw, but the whole fabric of your being will delight in the chain-breaking ceremony of moving from the bondage of other people's restrictions and limitations into the total independence of being YOU. Along the road of your journey, you will be treated to face-to-face encounters with all your Pharaohs'; and these lovers, spouses, bosses, and friends will wish to prevent you from becoming better, not only because now you must be acknowledged as an equal, but more so for the fact that you may prove to be an example to others. This restricts their future choices, thereby disrupting the delicate balance of fools and rulers!

January 7

*Love is on welfare in a cold heart*

Check this out. Love is particularly vulnerable in
any relationship where either or both parties have
poor credit histories with the store-house of their
emotions! If either is bankrupt emotionally, then
that person must extort feelings from the other in a
futile attempt to manage his or her own inadequacy.
This unwarranted emotional taxation often requires
adjustment to remedy the deficit because in any
situation where there is no return on a spent
commodity, whether it's a dollar or an emotion,
there is always a definite sense of loss. Learn to
trust in love and to reap its dividends
because lust is the inheritance tax on a love gone
wrong.

## January 8

*A man may argue his price---but never his place*
*-Ali-*

Ignore the charlatans and quacks. Give scant heed to the sages, but by all means, embrace the fools. Regarding the fool, it is always worth recalling that he should never influence what you wish to be, only that which you don't want to be. Since he is such a candid example of what not to be, feel free to emulate him in reverse.

*Jan. 9*
*It has been said that inspiration is 99%*
*perspiration. Well, perseverance is inspiration*
*without the perspiration. When you know you're*
*going to win----why sweat it!  -Ali-*

Perhaps it's best you understand now
Early on the reason for this talk
Really there's a big difference
Separating a true journey from a walk
Each day a real journey consumes you
Vigorously making you grow
Each day a walk just tires you
Rarely, barely making you go
Altitude rises during a journey's course
Nothing can change its sway
Charting your path to greater heights
Exposing the best of each new day.

## January 10

*The ABCs are the first fruits that knowledge extends to man's fertile mind. They are an intellectual springboard to wisdom and understanding. Use them wisely for they are investments. Squander them and you'll be unable to defend yourself against ignorance.      —ali-*

In any struggle for a new beginning, there will be limits placed upon your success if you don't possess a mastery of the language. This is critical. If I have something you want and you lack the skills to convey precisely what it is that you desire, then there is almost no chance of my filling your need. Your intent is not clear, so I don't understand you. What you must remember is that every closed door has its password, its secret knock, or a code that will open it. All you have to do is to learn how to say "open sesame" in the language appropriate to that particular door.  You can't expect the boardroom door to open for you if you speak "street" any more than you can look for apple seeds to produce oranges. Appropriate language must be used to fill the gap between a need and its resolution because the initial thrust of your power rests upon your ability to clearly ask for what you want.

## January 11

*Whenever you are out of touch with your own soul, it is then that you make house calls to the devil. – ali-*

Change does not happen in a vacuum. It is a part of a continuum, the dynamic process of becoming, peculiar to the evolution of human growth and development. As complex as change can oftentimes be, it will and can never be fully functional until you can successfully defend these gains against the mental "patron saints" of your former ways that will continue to be active as your transformation is becoming definite. During this interim period of self-discovery, you have to adjust to a new perspective in order to make the change effective. Just remember that when your heart approves, it is time to step out of the shadow of the "patron saints... Go wild... Lose yourself in the newness of YOU!

## January 12

*When you mean biz'ness, everything you do is a prayer.  –ali–*

But how should you pray? That depends on what you want. If you wanted a million dollars, then that might take a little more work because first you would have to pray to God to assist you in the development of your intelligence and talent so that you will be equipped to put yourself in a position to make that million dollars. So even before you start praying for a million dollars, you should already have asked the Creator to point out the talent by which He intends for you to earn your wealth. And then you beg Him to assist you in developing that skill, so you can put it to use to acquire that million. The money is available, but do you possess the skills to get it? In order to get something, certain other forces must be set in motion first. How are you going to be a great basketball player and you don't even have a ball? Wouldn't it make sense to pray for a basketball first? Don't pray for a big wedding when you don't even have a companion. Keep things in perspective. Not that God can't handle it, but so you won't get discouraged. When you stand on a close relationship with God, your prayer request will no longer seem like an appeal for foreign aid. It will simply be a blessing to go!

## January 13

*To be queen, what must be known is that it is not about the groove, but about the growth!*
*-ali-*

A sista's groove is that of all the people on the planet, she possesses the most idealized concept of the white man as a savior-in-waiting. For the older sistas, it's Jesus. To the sista in the hood, it's Uncle Sam with his 1$^{st}$ of the month welfare check; and to the young sista, it's Santa Claus. Better get hip. Girl, you have been a burden to carry and the white man ain't trying to rescue you. He is trying to lay your ass down!

## January 14

*The pillow is always softest when you're laying
your head where it shouldn't be.   —ali-*

This is a Sista Alert. There are no established
time frames where it will ever become permissible
for circumstance and condition to encourage you to
wake up and/or get wise.  This is a no-no that would
disrupt the orderly progression of your dependency
and hopelessness.   Your length of stay at the
threshold of being nonproductive is held to be the
amount of time necessary for you to dismiss  the lie
that procrastination does not hurt.

## January 15

*Watching yourself grow to heaven is much better*
*than waiting on yourself to go to hell*
                    -ali-

Get with this. On the way to you, you will have the privilege of watching yourself grow. As you bound outward from your sense of incompleteness, you will experience the ultimate joy of understanding how wonderfully growth heals. From this simple condition of self-evolvement, you will realize that personal growth is a thirst within you that strives to be enriched. Concentrate on it. You should also take note that attention to your inners ituation will offer loving companionship to the desires of your outer self. Every day on the journey is a renewed chance to interact with the beauty of becoming you, so stand on the horizon of each moment, and be awed by your own depth.

## January 16

*Don't be embarrassed. There is no need to be modest when the voice that does the bragging comes from within.   –ali–*

Don't launch yourself toward any goal, seeking to confirm  someone else's expectation because you can never be enhanced through the vicarious holding-on-to-someone-else's  dream.     Always recall vividly that you are not here as a gift to someone else's effort to live twice, or as a hobby for a mentor. You are here to inherit just those things that you need to become fully and wholly YOU. And for that-------there is no partnership. In contrast to the outer world, the inner sanctum is orderly and precise where the only voice heard is your own. Listen to this voice. All you will hear is how great you are.

## January 17

*Today is nothing more than a pat on the back.*
*Tomorrow is a hug and a kiss.  –ali-*

Tomorrow is always something more. It is a new season of hope where you are vested with a different chance to end a bad habit, start a new diet, or to fashion a better life.   Inside the fresh environment of a new day exists seeds of commitment. These seeds are the natural wonders of your inner world, and from them spring the vision under which you will labor to either despair, impair, or repair yourself. Don't you know that it is from your sense of purpose that your soul paints its self-portrait?   The universe will not award you anything until you possess an identity. The state of being only allows you the awareness of your senses. The art of becoming permits you to exercise them. In the larger perspective, it is not enough just to BE. The decision must be made to **BE MORE**! Give thanks to tomorrow by throwing it a "Baby shower" today. This is how you hug yourself with open arms

## January 18

*It is better to achieve than to receive    -ali-*

At every fork in the road on your journey to successful living, there are many distinctions to be made. One such distinction to be reckoned with is the line between what you ACHIEVE and what you RECEIVE. While there is never any uncertainty about what you receive, the same is not true with what you achieve since many people go through life filled with doubt about their achievements.  An achievement is the personal nourishment of your individual worth whereas receivership is merely the reassurance that you exist. Once you make the discovery of which is which, you will be able to understand the intricate synchronization between probabilities and possibilities, knowing which is a celebration of your merits and which is an invocation of chance. Don't make a career out of waiting-to-receive because sometimes the hand-outs stop. Explore the possibilities of your individual merit by achievement. It is a happy appointment with yourself.

## January 19

*Don't gamble----PLAN    -ali-*

Do you know how to detect failure?  Well, you can.  It is an acquired taste but you will always bring yourself closer to success when you realize that a plan is a bridge between your weaknesses and your potential. A good plan is much more that a high-chair for your ego.  It is an insurance policy against worry, a balm for doubt, and a healing for quitting.  PLAN. Don't worry about overdoing it because as long as you are comfortably aware of the dos and don'ts of your inner nature, you will prepare accordingly, but beware of your ego! If it is not firmly strapped in its booster chair, it can offer deceptive advice. To the ego, planning is like staging a party. Everything must be outrageous and exciting and colorful. Remember that when you reach the point where planning is fun, then you are no longer planning----you are gambling! And that's a whole 'nother story. PLAN
■■■■■■■■■■■■■■■■■■■■■■■■■■■■■■■■■■■■■■■■■■■

## January 20

*Your dreams can sometimes be a bad idea if you fail
to understand that oftentimes you are the biggest
enemy to their fruition.  —ali-*

Dig this. Make it a point to pay respect to your biggest foe----you!  This does not imply that you should honor the fact that your fears are sometimes the biggest obstacle to your advancement. Instead, it is the art of appreciating that success is a finely-crafted performance which is improved only with the constant refinement of you getting better on a day-to-day basis. Never lend support to your doubts, but keep your concerns in perspective. Learn when to turn a dream into a reality and when to let go of a bad idea. These are expressions of respect for yourself. They help you to get out of the way when you get in the way of the way you should be going to get there.
∎∎∎∎∎∎∎∎∎∎∎∎∎∎∎∎∎∎∎∎∎∎∎∎∎∎∎∎∎∎∎∎∎∎∎∎∎∎∎∎

## January 21

*A fact ain't nothing but an act that's been having
sex with a shot-caller    -ali-*

You have got to mean biz'ness! And that means moving from reaction to action because this is the way life behaves when there ain't no time for half-stepping.  Check out this episode. You *react* after the fact, but when you mean biz'ness, you have the juice to turn an act into a fact!  When you ain't got nuthin' coming but your last minute reactions to what others do to you, then you are simply tying a noose around your own neck!    ACT-----*and then watch your back!*  Always remember that it is much easier to get your back off the wall than it is to get a foot out of your ass! Correct the effect. Act in your own behalf!

## January 22

*Do you ever cross your mind?    -ali-*

You will never discover your potential, let alone express it sitting in the lotus position, chanting affirmations. All you will accomplish by this is the ability to exceed the expectations of your own capacity to both sell and buy yourself a dream. Until you learn how to stay afloat in the spiritual world, an affirmation is not an anchor, it is an anvil. When you know as much as possible about your desires to rise above the surprises, secrets, and scams of everyday living, you can cease bribing yourself with the small talk of affirmations, chants and promises because your inner voice will speak too you. That's the ticket.  Don't talk to yourself. Listen to yourself...

## January 23

*Prosperity is an unlimited provision that is manufactured by your potential but must be road-tested by positive action.*

−ali-

If it is your sincere desire to succeed, your greatest triumph will come if you realize that prosperity is an unlimited provision that is manufactured by your own potential. Black folks treat their potential with such confidentiality that no one else is even aware of its existence. For no apparent reason, of our own volition, we conduct ourselves as though we are bargain-hunters when it comes to living well. **STOP!!!.** You must understand that life offers no rock-bottom prices, and for the most part, existing only becomes a painful experience when you fail to assert your right to grab at all available opportunities. Don't be fooled. Positive thinking is only a good short-term investment in wishful day-dreaming if it is not road-tested by positive action. There's no escaping that science. Without positive action, positive thinking is sorta like a mental condom. It's protection, but it lacks projection. To be successful, you've got to get hip to the fact that you can't plant seeds of growth if the package ain't open.

## January 24

*There will be po' folks in hell also.   —ali-*

Do this. Repeat firmly:   *There is no spiritual equivalent to being well-off.*  This does not suggest that you have too lose your religion in order to get paid, but it does mean that you should scoff at the notion that poverty is a relative of piousness.  Don't buy that.  Jump ship now. The marketplace is not an occasion for wearing your wings.  Instead, you need either lawyers, guns, or money. And the willingness to go toe-to-toe with opportunists who trust religiously in coming-in-first.   It's nasty biz'ness, but there's good news.   You no longer have to suffer because of your spirituality. Know why? Just think about it like this, dear brotha or sista. Your spirituality is part of your domestic policy. Getting ahead is part of your foreign policy.  And people always get good at acting the fool when they are way from home. Heaven will wait.

## January 25

*Before you can score, you first have to know where the goal is.  —ali-*

Fuse this into your brain.  You have just one simple goal: to be the very best you can be at handling your own needs.  At all times, you should be working hard to boost your productivity to help and assist yourself in giving yourself whatever it takes to promote you to the next level.  However, you shouldn't get so busy that you miss one of the most amazing, significant developments of your individual progress. Namely, that you must step out into the frightening non-traditional role of standing up for yourself.  For once, you must make a point as a individual instead of a representative of an oppressed minority.  This one's for you.  This is rebellion, true, but it is also a central trend in being able to separate your needs from those of the herd. This is a major, profound assessment that cannot be ignored.  Us against them is a phony struggle until you have scored a victory in the real b battle of its "me-against-the-world"!

## January 26
*To imitate someone else is to deflate yourself.  –ali-*

Don't let smoke get in your eyes. You don't need to be a clone of someone else to get the job done.  This is a self-destructive vice, and you can never deliberately market your needs on the false assumption that if you buy a dream early enough and cheap enough, pay-back won't be so devastating. Wrong.  In this drive-by "needs-to-go" atmosphere of artificial mental addiction, it is usually true that your desire to follow in someone else's footsteps will always exceed any real need to. Therefore you   must set a goal of never losing custody of your identity because this is the direct pathway to your own path. Address yourself, and then dress yourself.   And while the garb of your own unique personality may not, at 1$^{st}$, fit you as well as designer jeans, you are incapable of ever getting too big for your britches.

## January 27

*Don't take no "shorts". Stop limiting yourself to merely coping with life via an obsession with survival tactics when the secrets of success are easier to learn.  –ali-*

Here's a tidbit for your own peace of mind, and it goes a little something like this. An intrinsic part of the over-all hype was to invade the consciousness of people of color and to restrict their vision. Why? Because by doing so, we would constantly remind ourselves that we are limited and limits, as such, always act as thirst-quenchers. They quench your thirst for what lies just over-the-rainbow. With no longing in your soul to keep you focused, getting "Shorted" becomes a seduction. You begin to welcome the opportunity of living, instead of the challenge of living well. You concentrate on survival rather that success. You commune with the sheer joy of existing, with no emphasis on how to make the experience worthwhile. This diminution is the natural habitat of a fool. Move! Migrate! Get Away! Don't live under the roof of hype. Begin a new relationship with your consciousness. Teach it that it has the sacred duty to make you laugh and rejoice. Self-employ yourself when it comes to what you allow yourself to see, think, do, and believe. Embrace the skillz needed to think for yourself. Lengthen and strengthen your vision. Go 4 what U know.
■■■■■■■■■■■■■■■

January 28
*See 4 yourself. Starting out with a good idea is a*
*damned good idea.   –ali–*

One something you shouldn't forget. You must forego the primitive impulse to be rude to yourself. While you may have learned that life favors the rich and the strong, you should never teach yourself that you can't be one of them.  Remember that the 1$^{st}$ step in leveling the playing field is an understanding of the terrain.  This means starting out with a good idea of what you are seeking for yourself.  Behind this elementary notion, you manage to turn prior defeats into "observation" lessons, eliminating the harmful effects of the "failure imperative", which coerces you to have nuthin' to do with success.  In fact, accessorize your attitude with the knowledge that there is no psychological necessity for you to sacrifice the beauty of living for the relative low cost of learning what not to do.  This is central to getting ahead because there may be a great number of times during the course of your life when you may not know what to do, but there should never exist a moment when you don't know what not to do.

## January 29

*Foolishness is the exotic mysticism of men who entertain themselves by looking into the flames of their "life candle" that burns at both ends.   –ali-*

Foolishness will have a deep impact on everything you do.   It is perhaps the greatest innovation the world has ever known.  As a result, foolishness will absolutely slow the pace of any advancements you may entertain. And it will always cause a considerable lapse between the long distance notion that you could possibly be reasonably successful at something, and the time it takes you to capitalize on that assumption. You are simply fattening yourself on self-induced methods to diminish your own efficiency.  No matter how much comic relief foolishness may provide after the fact, it is no exotic mysticism.  It is mental carnage.

January 30

*The good ol' boy system was made by men who enjoy making boys out of other men.  –ali–*

A final word of caution.  Details have been surfacing ever since black folks arrived in this country that the American dream is a nightmare if you don't cipher the thin line between *competition* and *regulation.*  Competition is the catalyst of getting by on the terms of your own merit, but if you constantly drop the ball in a game among peers and equals, chances are good that you are being regulated. It is the good ol' boy system at work and it works. On a personal level, regulation will tend to destabilize your chances of success. Be advised.  No trick was missed in the rush to stymie you, so learn that the difference between competition and regulation is so extreme because it was the game plan of those-in-the-know to cripple your chances of success.  As long as you are painfully underdeveloped mentally, you will never become a member of the club.  And that's a lily-white affair.
■■■■■■■■■■■■■■■■■■■■■■■■■■■■■■■■■■■■■■■■■■■■■■■■

January 31

*Remember that wringing your hands or simply sitting on your ass gives you the staying power to remain in the line of fire.  —ali-*

Here's a healthy dose of reality for ya.  You've got to have staying power.  Wanna know what that is?  Well, staying power is the painful experience of not wringing your hands or sitting on your ass when the going gets tough.  Staying power is the mantra of those who refuse to pull back when their optimism is initially buried beneath the warnings and threats of fair-weather friends or iron-clad foes. If you are tuff enough, staying power allows you a safety net because in the end your personal growth will usually be decided by how well you understand the lessons you have learned

## February 1

*Know your history or know hell   -ali-*

When you investigate the human drama of why some people are successful while others are not, you will be induced to accept the fact that African-Americans have never lost interest in becoming successful, but that other people have sought to invent a system where African-American success would be measured in terms of its value to them. We do not fail because we are spiritually, mentally or physically bankrupt. We fail because we were deliberately altered psychologically. We fail for precisely the same reason that the lions, tigers and bears from Ringling Brothers would fail if set free in their natural habitat. No matter how spectacular the victory, how often is it that the scantily-clad exploited cheerleaders share credit for the win? In America, people of color are and have been cheerleaders, kicking up our legs and dancing, providing halftime attraction in the game of life. We fail simply because we have been dispossessed

## February 2

*No man creates a slave to succeed him. Instead a slave is produced so that the master's son will be provided with a living example of his inherent superiority.  —ali-*

We stifle our children by fostering lies about the good tooth fairy, the Easter bunny, Santa Claus, etc. It was these lies, developed and nurtured in the public school system, that were primarily responsible for the miseducation of African-Americans past and present. From such incidental, seemingly harmless myths about   Santa Claus we spring boarded into the life-altering myths of white supremacy as invented by history books. At least, with the coming of age, black children get a good laugh at the joke pulled on them about the good tooth fairy, the Easter bunny, and Santa as they outgrow the lies, but unfortunately millions still cater to the myth of Good George (Washington), Honest Abe, and countless other worthless racially-inspired historical myths.  Remember this. At any point in the history of a country when a people can't find its own heroes in the history books, that people has been set up by that country to be slaves forever. Stand clear on this fact. We were set up to fail because no one produces a slave to succeed him!

February 3

*Affirmations without parity are like a bus without wheels. You can't get there from here.   –ali-*

When you realize that a complete system was put into place to serve as an obstacle to your success, you cannot be timid in your opposition to it, especially when you understand that every goal you seek to achieve during the entire course of your existence will be  affected. This should be a rallying point for all African-Americans from the brotha who wants to advance to Wall Street to the sista who wishes to lose weight because at the periphery of anything we attempt is the built-in limits naturally occurring via our mental rape. In the same way that physical rape can insure that a woman never trusts a man again, our mental  rape will also insure that we never trust our own success.

## February 4

*Don't complain-----change        -ali-*

So, there you have it. Everything you attempt to accomplish will be taxed by your attitude about yourself.   In any personal situation you may wish to call into being, whether shedding or gaining weight to shedding or gaining a mate or job, your mind is the instrument that will  have to be employed to move you toward the set goal. Therefore you have got to free your mind and the 1$^{st}$ step is to acknowledge that the Emancipation Proclamation    did    nothing    to    loosen    the psychological screws. You have got to face this fact, not to make peace with it. Until your mind is free from slave-like thinking, then your gains will continue to be minimal. We still are so awed by the invincibility of the white man's assumed superior thinking that we stymie ourselves. Have you ever heard of a successful slave?

## February 5

*Nature never plays it safe. In her kindness she will grant you a pacifier when you're ill, but she will also put you over her knee if you get too big for your britches. Either you follow her house rules or she'll tear the roof off the mother………*

*-ali-*

Nature has propounded many laws. One of these is the law of compensation. I call it nature's pacifier. When one organ of the body or limb is weakened, a corresponding organ or limb is strengthened in compensation. Thus, many who have weak eyes have stronger than usual hearing. People with lower body afflictions usually possess tremendous upper body strength. At any rate, when one system of the organism is weakened another is strengthened as compensation. Nature acts spontaneously. When nature acknowledged that the forces of our minds were diminished to such a degree that restoration was no longer possible, she awarded us a pacifier---a strong body! Our exquisitely, finely sculpted bodies, both male and female, only mirror the degree of our mental atrophy. Our wonderful bodies are nature's indictment against the rape of our minds. Our beautiful bodies bear witness against our diseased minds. Yes, we can outrun, out jump, and out-sport the white man, but we can't outthink him. A beautiful body entertains. A functioning mind produces. It's time to be weaned off the pacifier and to provide ourselves with real nourishment. Free your mind and your ass will follow!

## February 6

*Your body should be more that a plain brown wrapper for your passions and desires. It must be more than beautiful plumage that entices the eye, for the real power of a body lies in its ability to follow the commands of a well-ordered mind.* –
*ali-*

In the physical world, any time fair nature is defaced you can see the traces of the devastation that follows. There are fixed laws in the universe that cannot be abridged without longstanding, far-reaching implications. In essence, the same universal laws are in operation in the mental world and the traces of this devastation are clearly evident. All one must do is to heed the signs. Nature has left her insignia. The parallels of our mental rape are detailed clearly in the NFL and the NBA. These are the premier showcases for our beautiful bodies. Black men dominate here as bodies (players) but are noticeably absent as minds (coaches). We can entertain, but we can't produce. The consequences of this are evident when you look at the wealth transfer of sports. The bulk of the money goes to the owners. These are the superior minds that put the bodies through their paces. We're still sucking on our pacifiers.

## February 7
*Wrong touches everything wrongly.*
–ali–

We have beheld the problem and despite these setbacks, we can still plan for success. Moreover, the planning has to be sharply tailored to attack the core of the problem: mental repression and institutional racism. We must also accept as part of our collective healing that the damage was committed deliberately and with malice. As an individual, you must assess the full extent of your personal injury and to examine the breakdown against your individual history. Trace its detriment through your immediate family tree, measuring its adverse effects on your development as a person. Recall the lessons you were taught and the means by which you incorporated them into your thinking. Analyze your attitude towards yourself and others of the race. A clear pattern will emerge. If you are black in this country, you are the victim of a slave-making mentality which is so potent that it is the basis of failure even if you only desire cosmetic, superficial changes. The ghost of failure is present even if you seek to lose weight, stop smoking, quit cursing or any other little thing you do. That's how deep it goes. Wrong touches everything and everything it touches---it spoils.

## February 8

*A lie is a colorful snapshot of a man eating eggs when the hen ain't even started laying them.   –ali-*

Black folks applaud a good lie.  There should have been no way in hell you could wallow in the cold-hearted sentiment of the proverbial "all niggas are lazy and shiftless" myth, and then accept your own eyewitness account of your parents' hard toil to provide for you.  Every fiber of your being should have offered protest against this scalding lie as well as the countless others that belittle us as a people. Thus began our spiritual psychosis. . O black man and black woman, behold the damage done to us by this country's lies.

February 9

*Your mind is a garden where you plant the seeds from which your fears grow. You sow them in the top soil of your ignorance, water them with your tears, cultivate them in your heart, and then wait on them to grow big enough to eat you. Ali-*

Think. Go back. Find your lie or your myth. Each of us has a specific lie or myth that is the instrument of our own personal defeat. This is the thread from which everything else is built. Find it. Destroy it. Heal. What prominent deception has set you up for failure: "niggas ain't shit", "red women are evil", "you ain't got enough sense to pour piss out of a boot", "you ain't good for nuthin', "you just like your daddy", etc. In sum, when nothing more is heard from your lie then it can no longer dominate your future, and the rest of the system that has been put in place to check your progress will fall away. You have removed the central support beam. Your outlook will change.

## February 10

*A cure always sounds good when you're reading it*
*off the prescription bottle.   –ali-*

Getting your life well is no house party.  It is a search and destroy mission aimed at eliminating any weakness that sickens you. You cannot take it for granted that you are going to get better simply because you know what's wrong.   You are at war. Your voice has been raised in protest. Weakness must be crushed.  Don't civilize your weakness by nursing and babysitting it like many smokers hoping to quit do, reducing their dependence gradually. Welcome the pain----and quit.  There is no need to adopt  any second-hand ideas about pain. Yes, it hurts like hell......Persevere!

## February 11

*Go! But first clear the path.  –ali-*

Using the take-no-prisoners approach, you can throw off your chains. Trying to improve your conditions under a less organized program will do little or nothing. CHARGE!  It is vital to come within arms' length of your shortcomings and then strike. This way you feel your own power. You get consumed by the rush of dismantling your own fears. You will demand victory. CHARGE! Power is balm for the oppressed man's soul. Go forth boldly. CHARGE!

## February 12

### *Cute is not a cure*
*-ali-*

The black woman in America is under the reprimand of her own vanity. She has informally adopted "being pretty" as a feminine cure-all for much that is wrong in her life. An affirmative nod from the mirror is a seeming sedative against feelings of hopelessness, depression, or sadness. Being cute gives her the unrestricted right to be naive. Her makeup makes up for her inability to see things as they actually are, and this apparent loss of vision only fortifies the distance between what she can and cannot accomplish. This individualized purchase of "cosmetic" freedom is like paying money to a system that compels you to feel you are not beautiful enough. You better face it, girl, the mirror ain't nuthin' but a cash register in disguise.

February 13

*A smile is the transfer of wealth from your heart to*
*your head        -ali-*

There is a duality in the universe that is dangerous
to ignore. There is good/evil; pretty/ugly;
winners/losers, etc. They all belong to a delicate
infrastructure of balance where the development of
one occurs naturally due to the existence of the
other. How could we truly measure beauty if there
was not ugly by which to compare it? Everything is
adjusted on this scale of balance, so don't delude
yourself, Don't lose your perspective. See your
world for what it is, and don't allow kings, priests,
or presidents to mislead you. The world is
sometimes not so beautiful. Call a spade a spade

February 14

LUV

## February 15

*The size of the gift does not always indicate your true value. Sometimes it's simply a clue as too how much you're worth not knowing how valuable you actually are.*                    *-ali-*

On Valentine's Day, the wife measures herself by the size of the gift received from the husband. She regards her worth as commensurate with her man's ability to spend money on her. The more money he spent, the better she feels. And that's because in America, money is the social invention by which our value is established, especially when it comes to someone spending it on us. Dig that. Now, in view of this, I assert that we, Africa-Americans, are indeed very damned important! Did you know that the white man has spent billions of dollars on us? Why? Because we're special. And he knows it. That's the reason why he has spent billions of dollars revising, rewriting and doctoring history! He has put more money into this effort than he has spent on NASA. We are so important that he spent billions of dollars to cover up the truth of our magnificent achievements. He rewrote history to write us out of it.

■■■■■■■■■■■■■■■■■■■■■■■■■■■■■■■■■■■■■■■■■■■■■

## February 16

Skillz is skillz. If you got enough game to make a sista sell her body, then you got the skillz to influence her to get an education.S —ali-

A system of success demands a definite shifting of your priorities and with the required self-adjustments, the need to end the debilitating misuse of your talent. We have permitted our talent to be assigned inferior status in order to justify the wide spectrum of lies and myths that rule the marketplace. What dictates unequal pay for equal work? Racism.....and the constant selling of our talent cheaply. This has proven to be one of the greatest economic tragedies dealt out to us, forcing us to become the hoes of the marketplace. Dig this! Two boys, one black, one white, apportioned with the same automotive skillz and driving ability will employ their talent in vastly different ways. The white boy will grow up to be a NASCAR driver, the brotha a getaway driver for a stick-up crew. A brotha with skill in advertising does not advance to Madison Avenue, he moves to the corner becoming a dope boy. This is a drastic misuse of talent, and as a consequence, scores of black men have been consumed by the fire of this pathos. The same skillz that it takes to market and sell a bag of dope can be used to sell books. The hip-hop nation must really get hip. Stay tuned.

February 17
*The homeless beggar when he finds a dollar upon the sidewalk does not stop to ponder whether a drug-dealer or a preacher lost it. He simply uses it to his benefit and is thankful.*          *–ali–*

The hip-hop nation must move towards real success, in sum, by christening their hybrid industries with legitimacy.    One of the great weaknesses of the underground economy is that it has failed to promote itself in the real marketplace by reforming itself commercially. Don't flinch at this because virtually every bastion of American capitalism sits atop a crime. Trace the fortunes of any or all of the leading wealthy families of this country and see the blood on their hands. It's just that the "robber barons" were criminal visionaries who used their dirty money wisely and learned to hide behind the façade of respectability.   Brothas stumble because they attempt to make crime a career.   Realistically, the crime is merely or should be a short-term job opportunity.   The career begins where the crime ends ▪▪▪▪▪▪▪▪▪▪▪▪▪▪▪▪▪▪▪▪▪▪▪▪▪▪▪▪▪▪▪▪▪▪▪▪▪▪▪▪▪▪▪▪▪▪▪▪

## February 18

*Until you include batteries to power it up, the vote is merely a useless plaything.    —ali-*

Short-sighted planning and thinking will forever pose a formidable obstacle to our success, individually and collectively.   The rumored assertions that things will get better on their own or that we have countless options only buttress our inability to pull ourselves up by our own bootstraps. As surprising as it may seem, we're running out of options. On the one hand, the efforts we've attempted have been riddled by divisiveness. On the other hand, the efforts were band-aid -like in their approach, like trying to prepare for surgery out of a first-aid kit. In nearly every instance----failure. These are times when drastic measures are called for. We must put all available resources to work. We no longer have to be powerless as a people. Come together.

## February 19

Prisons are miniature Americas that devour black flesh and then regurgitates the remains to feed her young. –ali-

On the national level, black men are a most lucrative export crop. Through their confinement and due to it, the prison industry is booming. A black man extracted from the inner cities provides substantial wealth to a prison industrial complex that feeds on them. And you think they want to end the drug trade? By no means. As long as the market remains strong, both the government and Wall Street are going to keep counting dollars. Be advised that the government is not loyal to any agenda to support our success in this country. Isn't the trend clear by now?

## February 20th

*One man's misery is another man's money* -ali-

Our collective successes cannot be built upon the small expanding base of individual businesses headed up by professional athletes' and cinema personalities mainly because these businesses as such are geared for personal financial enhancement. Additionally, it must be noted that there is a vast difference between starting a business and creating job opportunities.

Our economic longevity must be supported by the latter. Our money does not circulate in our communities, allowing everyone to benefit from it.

Instead, it is immediately sucked out into the hostile white economy. We must turn the wolves away from our cabbage patch and refuse to funnel our profits out to them without our having made good use of it, receiving full value for our dollar. To succeed economically, we must exert full control over our finances. We can't get fooled again.

## February 21st
### *A name is the face of your existence*
#### -ali-

All things considered, perfection is not intimate knowledge conferred upon a man simply because he deems himself worthy of success. Moreover, power is revered strategy backed by both worldly and spiritual laws. Of a certainty, man must love self, but this ideal can never be attained to and will forever remain a fruitless pursuit until a man honors the value of his name. The significance of this shouldn't be understated or its intrinsic relevance diluted. Names are our most definitive characteristic and yet African-Americans, of all people on the planet, lack our own identification as we still carry the names of those who owned us. There is strength in a name with meaning. Since our "import" names mean nuthin", is it any wonder why we resort to nicknames to identify us? It demonstrates a search for self that is not entailed in our so-called given names. In the case of almost any nickname, the individual strives hard to live up to his moniker. Slick will be slick. Mad Dog will conduct himself as such. Killer will be on the prowl to become worthy of his title. Haven't you every noticed how people take fierce pride in living up to the ideal embodied in their nicknames? If not convinced, simply investigate the phenomenon. Who wants to be guilty of perpetrating a fraud? By bestowing upon your child a meaningless name, you surrender the ability to fashion his attitude and outlook so he'll have to take his cue from a nickname. You blow your very first chance to shape your child for success. When your child has a name indicating greatness and you instill him/her with the importance of this attribute, he/she will earn the right to wear it. A name is the very 1st gift you give your child, so start them off strong! Love them by name.

February 22

*A man who has lived well requires no fancy epitaph on his tombstone. All that need be said is that he lived up to his name.*

-ali-

A name is the spiritual seat of your being. It rises up from deep within the soul of your essence and colors your attitude about yourself. An individual peers out from behind the eyes of a name in much the same way your physical eyes stare out from your face. Your name is the visible component of your aspirations. It is a constant yardstick by which you are eternally monitored. You are perennially made aware of where you stand in relation to the rest of the world by how close you approximate your name. To make a woman a queen, it is important that you first call her one.

# February 23

*O black woman, heed this secret well. If you want to know if a man will make a good husband, don't check his bank account or the fire in his sexual endowment. Simply measure the distance between him and his name.*
*–Ali-*

The pressure of not having a meaningful name may seem a weak point, but it shows mass support for the idea that we, as a people, cared very little about living without the tacit approval of our former slave masters. We so imprison ourselves by our identification with our former owners that we continue to carry the stigma of his name. Usually upon a divorce, the woman immediately casts off her husband's name in order to totally free herself from all reminders of that relationship. Many developing countries upon gaining independence from foreign rulers don't hesitate to change the name of their country in an attempt to clearly demonstrate that they are no longer owned. The entire theory of freedom revolves around the notion of breaking fresh ground and living better. The very kernel in this seedling is to identify your independence by name. When a ho liberates herself from prostitution, she will go to great length to let you know that the label no longer applies to her. She realizes that her moral resurgence is safeguarded by the fact that you no longer identify her as a ho since she is now free. This benign, inexcusable neglect on our part alerted the ruling class that we were just whistling Dixie because to gain freedom and then to maintain the names of our bosses was laced with latent pacification

# February 24

*A miscast vote is like casting your pearls before swine.*
-Ali-

While traveling the path of life, sometimes your feet may slip because you only see the crust of things and not the crux of things. Sometimes you become absorbed in a program or institution that has no more merit than its opposite but due to the aggressive cult personality of one particular individual you get hooked into a system without exploring alternatives. That's why in the early days the majority of black people were Republicans. Abe Lincoln's birthday was just a few days ago, but this is by no means a nod to that occasion. It merely suggests our long-time willingness to tag along and invent leaders who don't serve our best interests. African-Americans adopted the Republicans because it was the party of Mr. Lincoln... Lincoln didn't free any slaves! Lincoln didn't sign the Emancipation Proclamation out of moral certitude, he did it out of dire necessity, even saying repeatedly that his intent was to save the union and that if he could do it without freeing the slaves------he would. Some great Emancipator. He cared nothing about the status of slaves, yet we still hold him up in emulation. Today, we're Democrats out of this same ignorance and we still stand in bondage as presidents have imitated Lincoln by signing papers that purport hope, but carry no provisions to enforce that hope.

## February 25

*When you bury your heroes, make sure it's the man*
*and not his ideas that you kick sand on. —Ali-*

Oftentimes the failure of a person or people can be established not only by the quality of the leader whose tenets he or they espouse, but also by the significance they pay to their_historic moments. One must always honor their history regardless of the circumstances which spawned it No person of Jewish descent has ever been asked to downplay or to forget the Holocaust, yet blacks are constantly chided in public and in private to disregard slavery as if it doesn't still impact us today. White people honor their heroes beyond the grave. That's why Elvis is still so vital today. Every white kid knows about the Beatles and their contributions to rock and roll. White radio stations have a "Beatles for Breakfast" format where the music is kept alive. On the other hand, how many black kids know about the Temptations, the premier R&B group? Their awesome accomplishments are never noted or promoted. We abandoned jazz and the blues, music we originated, and we throw away our culture in an attempt to crossover into mainstream society. That is an expression of self-hatred as visible as the wearing of blue contact lens. How can we ever succeed if we are guilty of self-hatred? We flee from our history as though it will expose us to greater infamy. We'd rather pretend when what we need to do is to wake the hell up!

## February 26

*Your child may never grow up to be a chemist, but believe me, the home will surely be his laboratory. The child is your microscope. Whatever you do in private will be magnified by him in public.*
*–Ali-*

In the same manner that the body can heal itself naturally, you can heal yourself of the failure malaise, but there must be a syllabus for success and it must be designed to meet your personal needs. Of immense importance also is that your re-education be structured so that it provides instruction for your children as well. The involvement of your children in your success (or drive towards that success) must be compulsory as this will acquaint them with the lessons that have rewarded you. This proximity will reinforce their belief in your worth and capability while at the same time dispelling any notion that what you have achieved is via tokenism or set asides. As they are a witness to your success, hard work and discipline will be dignified in their eyes and the science of victory will find a place in their hearts. When your child does not have a hand-in-hand acquaintance with success, then it is unthinkable to assume he won't fail. Without either lessons or examples, he can't even be expected to become even nominally successful because success rarely occurs independent of strong desire. Great advances can be made when success is a household word.

## February 27
*Nurture your nature by being natural.*
-ali-

Nature vs. nurture. That is the eternal question, but if you have your thinking cap on, you won't need a "street" degree to cipher which course is the right one. So dig this.

All men, whether from Harvard or the "Hood" are fashioned from the raw components of what nature has inherently bestowed upon us as human beings and what we are nurtured on as citizens of our neighborhoods. No man, no matter how smart or strong, can escape the conditioning influences of what I call the "Dynamic Duo". They constantly provide the fuel that stokes the fire of your baptism, granting you a full access pass to either heaven or hell. On the one hand, nature has equipped us with a built in success quotient and since the Creator knows precisely who we are, he has provided us with the tools required to meet, greet, and beat adversity. On the other hand, however, is the hood, a cruel Pharaoh who compels men to make bricks without straw? Something the hard knock education of the hood is so traumatic and devastating that it acts as a block, a red light stuck on stop. When your experiences are so petrifying that they override your natural potential, then you effectively become a candidate for the ghetto graveyard, a mental cemetery where there is no hope. Don't go there. Don't let the hood make you hood.

## February 28

*8Your child will never become acquainted with his God-like qualities if his fears scare the devil out of him.          —Ali-*

Your child will never be able to order his priorities without first girding himself in the fundamental belief that God is all that he should fear. This belief must exist as the cornerstone of his ethics, and his moral foundation must be layered on top of this truth because it will, at once, free him from the puny fear of man.  Once he absolves himself of the fear of man, then his opportunities will forever remain unlimited because he will conduct himself as an equal and bow to no man. The fear of God should influence your child, not the fear of man. Your child must be supercharged with this knowledge for there is no secondary or alternative wisdom to compensate for its lack.  All other roads lead to doom.

## *March 1*

*Sunshine is a dimple on the cheeks on morning*
-Ali-

Spirituality is not a phantom notion. On several occasions during the course of your life, you will be compelled to search for the reason why you're haunted by the phenomenon of 'being dead yet alive'. It is the hysterical child of an emotionless soul. You must not nurture it. Without preamble, you must feed your soul the song of the birds, the flight of the bumblebee, and the smell of roses. Open the window and let the fresh blast of creation in. Your cure rests with the ease by which you commune with God. Nature is God's dialogue.
Talk back by participating in the jubilation of nature.

*March 2*
*Your eyes may christen it, your heart may desire it,*
*but it ain't love until your head lies down beside it.*
-Ali-

You cannot petition the empty soul for love!
Affections are the festive patrons of a happy heart and they cannot reside in the tenement of a dilapidated slum. Love is the philosophical questioning of your soul; the chubby, baby-faced soulful chatter that asks if you're ready to be experienced, and then performs a wedding ceremony between your heart and your head.
The heart and head must be in synch first or else you will expect too much and give too little.
Your heart will seduce you with promises
while your head will induce you to wait for further instructions. The heart is composing poetry. The head is doing math. When you're able to pair your heart and your head, you will find the balance that allows you to grow into the love that is offered, and to expand its boundaries from within.
Affections are highly opportunistic. They just need a place to call home.

*March 3*
*Don't allow your memory of love to become a*
*deterrent to love.*
-Ali-

To get ahead in love, you must stop making outpatient visits to the experiences of your prior relationships since the comparisons could prove fatal to the enjoyment and nurturing of the relationship at hand. We are so fragile that we feel as if we can't escape heartache so we are on constant guard for its approach. This is premeditated fear. And perhaps the reason you witness its return is not because of characteristic symptoms-----but characteristic responses! Without a doubt, the universal, characteristic response to fire is the natural pulling back of the hand. Check yourself. Don't compare the responses of others until you have checked your actions first. No matter how beautiful the flame, who wants to get burned?

## March 4

*Luv is your heart and your head working on a groove theory.   –Ali-*

No matter what you see in your mate or expect to receive as compensation for your expended emotions, love is essentially a blind date until your heart and head come to terms.  They must work in unison on a regular basis, computing and analyzing harmless "miscues" rather than assessing them against the relationship's chances of survival. At the onset of too many relationships, the focus is misplaced. Instead of concentrating on extracting pleasure from the relationship, the concern is with avoiding pain.  This keeps your defenses up, and can at times block the love. So let down your guard, keep your focus out of the past, and love the one you're with...

## March 5

*No man should compel himself to contend for the attention of a woman who has too high an opinion of herself.* -Ali-

Have you ever seen the type of woman so steeped in conceit that she feels it is somehow therapeutic to love her? The deception is so consuming that she doesn't think to give anything to the relationship. She expects it to gather steam simply under the labor of the man's slavish devotion to her. When a woman's opinion of herself is too high, and all she brings to the affair is her physical beauty, then the travel time between hello and goodbye is bound to be short. Great physical beauty while alluring is not emotionally sufficient ground to support a lasting relationship because everything will be viewed in the light most favorable to upholding her ego. A man, no matter how valiant he is, can never succeed in a relationship where he must win a woman's ego instead of her heart.

## March 6<sup>th</sup>

*The funny thing about love is that you earn from it
just what you have leaned from it.*

-Ali-

When love is new, your emotions are like school
children on a trip to the zoo. Everything beckons,
glowing with sunshine, pulsing with joy. This is a
freebie. It can be savored, pored over, luxuriated in,
and devoured without guilt. Once it's gone these
moments cannot be salvaged. They were merely
attention-getting sensory modifiers whetting your
appetite for more, but the rest comes with strings
attached. You have to work for them. You now are
required to plumb the depths of another person's
soul to extract emotions. It is not impossible work if
you are perceptive. The love is there. Waiting. Get
it. And feel good. It will be even better now because
you have earned it, and know that the trick is not so
much in trying to keep love new, but in making it
last.

## March 7

*Lust is the painful inflammation of your heart brought on by the eating of forbidden fruit that causes congestion in your head.*     *–Ali-*

Lust is not love. Lust is the momentary loss of good sense where your head does not comprehend what your heart is doing. Unlike love, lust is completely unaware of any justification for its existence after sex, and that is the reason for the after-the-act guilt. Lust leaves no foundation to build upon so it is nothing more than a disciplinary sanction that you impose upon your future right to develop a monogamous relationship. Beware that lust is aberrant behavior, and even though you may perceive yourself to be "sexually insane" during the commission of the act, you still are guilty of stealing something that does not belong to you.

## March 8

*Sometimes when your body parts get out of control, a broken heart is oftentimes the agony of de-feet not moving quickly enough to keep your head from between your legs.*    *—Ali-*

A broken heart is the appropriate penalty for the misappropriation of your emotions, and it is a serious violation of nature to attempt love when there is no pre-existing respect for the power and beauty of it. The law of your own being will not permit you to straddle the fence between love and lust for long before your head criticizes the foolishness of your heart. You can nearly always delegate lust, employing it in the service of your weakness, and it will perform under any stimulating settings no matter how inconsistent with what you know is right as long as there are no provisions for commitment. You choose to participate in lust because it is an inviting solicitation to the proverbial "getting somethin' for nuthin'" idea, but what you don't recognize is that it enhances your inability to abolish this habit when someone truly wants to love you. As a result, you promote your own chances of a broken heart. When you learn to respect the power of love, your emotions will stop hitting you below the belt.

■■■■■■■■■■■■■■■■■■■■■■■■■■■■■■■■■■■■■■■■■■■■■

## March 9

*Don't wreck----spot check!*      *-Ali-*

Don't neglect to spot check yourself. Never underestimate the power of estimation. This prevents avoidable and unjustified judgment errors as well as stops you from devaluing any of your strengths. It is a mental relationship that puts and keeps both your strengths and weaknesses in perspective. The spot-check is especially warranted before you approve yourself worthy of making a binding decisions of the moment. In all situations, cost and loss must be calculated because they are the features that determine winners and losers. So don't wreck----stop-check.

## March 10

*Ain't much of an escape plan when you trying to run with your pants down 'round your ankles? –*
*Ali-*

You cannot profit from love if you skim your emotions. Being in love is not a charity where you only donate what you don't need or no longer have any use for. Your emotions are like couriers and you can recruit them to do your bidding, but first you must have some idea of what love is. You cannot succeed in love if your emotions are instructed to endorse or negotiate a short-term contract. This is subject to failure because to love means holding nothing in reserve. It is self-defeating to a relationship to enter into it with ½ your heart willing to commit while the other half is developing an escape plan. Practice love without limit... Don't be fooled by false hunting signs that insist that love is seasonal or automatically subject to the discretion of whomever comes along next with ½ a heart to invest in a feel-good-quick scheme. Love is doing it with your heart on 10.

## *March 11*

### *They just make "pretty" failures.*
#### -Ali -

Why is it that so many somehow buy into the fallacy that beautiful people conceivably possess special skills when it comes to love? We willingly assume that as a supplement to their good looks, they are gifted with strong technical skills that will personally allow them to skirt heartache without taking any of the usual precautions. Not hardly true. Like everyone else they cannot approach their emotions with the unsupervised freedom to mismanage them, and neither are they awarded any specialized knowledge of how to make love work or last. All they have access to is the inherent ability to verify their need to be loved, and then to satisfy that need through the agency of someone wise enough to know the difference between love and lust. Ditto for the rest of us, too.

■■■■■■■■■■■■■■■■■■■■■■■■■■■■■■■■■■■■■■■■■■■■■■■■

March 12<sup>th</sup>

*When pleasure is at work, there is usually heaven as
an endorsement, but always there's Hell to pay.*
*-Ali-*

In its very early stages, lust is oftentimes able to avoid detection due to the false information your head is getting from your heart, and it is at this juncture where one is most easily convinced to act foolishly. The pleasure principle is at work. The pleasure center of your brain has the unsophisticated task of stimulating you, and it will defraud you into believing that if it feels good to you it has to be good for you. As the chief trustee of this obligation, it will pass out messages that may qualify you for instant gratification that do not take into account the nature of the risks or the impending consequences. Pleasure does not dabble into the implications of morality or ethical considerations. That is not part of its job description. Its only duty is to counter pain and it is a mercenary when it comes to getting the job done. Pleasure is a stake. No matter how hard it may seem, it is always safe to identify your feelings and to introduce them to common sense. Love will verify itself.

## March 13

*Don't simply tell your children about love, teach them about love.     -Ali-*

You may have no desire to hear this, but love is essentially worthless until you learn how to appreciate it. Until you recognize this you will never be aware of the threat you subject yourself too emotionally by attempting to love by default. It's like a beautiful car in the yard with no keys.

## March 14

*Lies are eyes in the back of your lover's head.  –*
*Ali-*

Nothing chills your right to exist in a happy relationship quicker than a lie, especially your common day-to-day habits and actions that  make a finding against you. **HOW CAN I BELIEVE YOU LOVE ME WHEN YOU TREAT YOURSELF IN A RECKLESS FASHION?** Your whisper of love is found inadequate if you smoke, drink, get high, eat unwisely, or engage in any other unhealthy acts... This is clear proof that you don't love yourself, so how in the hell can you love someone else?  Your involvement in an unwholesome lifestyle constitutes a lie against your ability to truly love someone else because it is apparent that you're only in the relationship, not so much for love as for pleasure. That's the same reason you smoke, drink, get high------it makes you feel good.  Recognize the lie that bears daily witness against you. Also remember that loving yourself makes loving somcone else easier.

## March 15

*You're in the wrong emotion when you simply expect 'something' out of love. It's designed to give you everything.    —Ali-*

Another reason why we get such low grades when it comes to love is that we group it according to its returns, which in actuality demonstrates our attempts to measure love. This grouping process allows us to expect "something" from love instead of everything. Sadly, We ruin the underlying power of the emotion because love will not conform to charts, graphs or mathematical calculations.    No matter how wonderful you are in either the bedroom or the kitchen, don't disqualify love by challenging it or chaining it to a timetable. See tomorrow's Snapshot...
■■ ■ ■ ■■■■■■■■■■■■■■■■■■■■■■■■■■■■■■■■■■■■ ■

## March 16

*For the sake of love, love what love is.*
*-Ali-*

Love is the affirmative showing of the heart's all inclusive ability to give everything, being unable to hold anything back or in reserve. Love's existence depends upon its maximum exposure to that which inflames it. Love is all that the emotion can be. LOVE IS. Love will not exhaust itself. When you examine the "loves" of your life, if you can make a clear distinction between them, then you have not loved wholeheartedly. They all should have been loved equally and that is "all out", no limit. That's how love establishes itself. Don't control the potential of love. It performs best when working in excess of any maximum you may think there may be.
■■■■■■■■■■■■■■■■■■■■■■■■■■■■■■■■■■■■■■■■■■■■■■■■

## March17

*Don't let the status quo compete with your*
*happiness quotient.*
*-Ali-*

Is there such a thing as a happiness quotient? In determining the precise amount of joy you deserve during the course of your life, what factors should be considered? While the responses may vary due to individual uniqueness, there must also be allowances made for the timely changes that age will impose upon your altered viewpoint as you approach the foreseeable future in a rapidly changing society. Also know that your personal happiness will be corroborated by your individual wisdom. Go for it. There is no threshold...

■■■■■■■■■■■■■■■■■■■■■■■■■■■■■■■■■■■■■■■■■■

March 18

*Happiness is more private than public.* –ali-

Some people foolishly expect happiness to be some high-octane public announcement of how great things are or should be when happiness, in general, is more of a quiet response to all the things you have done right.

## March 19

*Sometimes the whisper at night will become a
scream the morning after.*
-Ali-

When it comes to sex, you do not act meaningfully towards yourself if your primary concern is with whether he will respect you in the morning. Your concern should be more consistent with your interest in whether he respects you before the act! Sex under pressure, no matter how subtle, is the verbatim whisper of his intentions screaming BITCH!

## March 20

*You don't have sufficient skills 2 hoodwink
Father Time*
-Ali-

You should understand that sometimes time will invoke change upon your relationship. Oftentimes, the preferred practice of time is to impose sanctions upon the relationship when you entertain improper behavior such as thoughtlessness, forgetfulness, and boredom. Then the relationship assumes the character of "your body's here with me but your mind is somewhere else". In truth, it is not wholly time that is the culprit but moreso the changes wrought by time.

## March 21

*Let it pass if it doesn't suit your plans.*
*-Ali-*

What is it about change that makes it such a home wrecker? Foremost is the fact that it imperils  private, personal conduct and requires it to be observed under the authority of "updates." The implicit consent <u>of</u> once accepted behavior  now becomes suspect. This is nothing more than change begging us to reconsider earlier opinions. Remember when it was cool simply to have sex. No more. Now, you've got to freak! Still, change is not to be demonized. Simply be aware of it and view it in light most favorable to your relationship. If it doesn't promote felicity at the address, then exercise the option to let it pass.

## March 22

*Change is time on the installation plan*
-ali-

Some people are deemed foolish enough that they desire to bask in the experience of every change. They are thrill-seekers. They insist on experimenting with every change as if it is some exotic drug even when they don't perceive the nature of the change. They explore the merits of change for no valid reason. Change is the natural consensus of time which does not need our personal support to sustain itself. Also, if change is not a credit to your betterment--- then don't change.

■■■■■■■■■■■■■■■■■■■■■■■■■■■■■■■■■■■■■

## March 23

*When love comes to town, go early and get a good seat. Sometimes the curtain comes down after the first act.*  *—ali—*

Sometimes, you may not get to go. The glow of love  so powerfully suggests itself as an endorsement for eternal happiness that we abandon our rights and duties as guardians of sane thinking. We readily allow ourselves to conjure up childhood fantasies of romance. In the beginning, your heart will articulate a bold challenge, speaking out brazenly in behalf of its own competency to make love last forever, but as time passes, some will surely know: They can't get there from here. LET GO.  Despite failure to meet your childhood fantasy. LET GO. You are not completely diminished. LET GO. If the love is gone and there is nothing to hold on for, let go because holding on will only harden your heart. LET GO!

## March 24

*Loneliness is love with its hat on backwards*
*-ali-*

Think about this. Even though love is a form of self-defense against loneliness, you can never ultimately conclude that there is either a social or historical reason to believe that loneliness will not sometimes win through. The most troubling thing about loneliness is that it is so patient, so controlled. All it does is wait. You never have to search for loneliness, but you are burdened with the task of keeping it away. No matter who you are or where you are, abuse love and loneliness is there. And it will not go away on its own. Remember this: While love may up and leave, loneliness never will! The moral of this Snapshot is: You must either learn how to make love stay or how to make loneliness go.

## March 25

Loneliness is love with its hat on backwards
Opening the door for pain
Never knowing when or how to leave
Entering inside your brain
Listening in on your private heartache
Inviting himself to stay
Nodding his head and popping his fingers
Eager to dance and play
Soon your heart is a desolate place, no dwelling home for joy
Such is the way of loneliness when love is treated like a toy.
∎∎∎∎∎∎∎∎∎∎∎∎∎∎∎∎∎∎∎∎∎∎∎∎∎∎∎∎∎∎∎∎∎

*March 26*

*When you can test your love, it is not the best of love*
*-ali-*

You become eligible for loneliness when you can measure and evaluate the substance of your love by how long it's been since the last time you had reason to smile. If the account of your smiles is disproportionately lower than your frown account, then guess who is coming to breakfast? Good morning Heartache

*March 27*

*Hello is sometimes good bye in waiting*
*-ali-*

In parting, breaking up should not be a malicious get-back scheme to wreak as much havoc on the other party as possible. Please recall that goodbye must be underlined by (1) a clear and precise reason for the breakup that is acknowledged by both parties, (2) a concerted attempt to rectify, correct or to amend the cause of the breakup (3) failing to rectify, correct or to amend the cause, a review to investigate whether or not the cause can be forgiven and lived down, (4) the opportunity to part if not as friends, never as foes. At the very least, this will create an atmosphere conducive to your heart's convalescence and speedy recovery.

## March 28

*Always leave a light on in your heart. You never know when a weary traveler may be seeking refuge.* —ali—

Any argument that love is loneliness waiting to happen must be soundly rejected because it invalidates the individual health and wellbeing of your heart. In order to preserve the integrity of love, you must not offer sympathy to loneliness by loving carelessly. Technically, as soon as any relationship begins, there exists the reasonable likelihood it won't last, but this still doesn't grant you the luxury to love as though it won't.

## March 29

*When you make provisions to be somebody's baby, you must not straddle the fence between your heart and your heart.*

*–ali–*

Keep this in mind. The mere presence of your heart at the site of love is not enough of a guarantee to move past hello because your head may fail to appreciate the significance. How can your head be substantially influenced or swayed when no precautionary measures have been taken to cure the defects of prior errors made by the heart? The heart heals. The head doesn't. And it remembers. Remember that to the head, all pain is cause for a full alarm since it recognizes no distinguishing quality as degree. Simply put, all pain must be avoided because the head will damn sure protect itself. STOP.LOOK.LISTEN. LEARN!
■■■■■■■■■■■■■■■■■■■■■■■■■■■■■■■■■■■■■■■■■■■■■■

March 30

*Luv is the gateway through which the heart must*
*pass*
*-ali-*

In certain rare situations after a breakup, the heart deliberately withdraws, emphasizing its stubborn reluctance to love again. It gives visible notice of its unavailability by placing its emotions beyond the reach of feeling. However, this is uncommon. The usual practice of the healing heart is to start again. After a breakup, there is no expiration date or no deadline that must be met before the heart defaults. So don't rush. To rebound into instant physical involvement as a primary attempt to remedy pain is begging for problems. While it may be technically satisfying for a moment, you will never be able to overcome the guilt of knowing that the relationship was conceived as an anesthetic. U don't have to go there. Breaking up is not the end of the road. Oftentimes, it is merely the fork in the road.

## March 31

*Never seek companionship through the eyes of someone else.*
*-ali-*

When you are ready to try love again, there should be no other more truly conclusive demonstration of that fact than that you are ready. It is not essential to personalize your concerns that your children may not be agreeable or that your boss is demanding more of your time. It is not even justifiable to concede to your anxiety. If you recognize the time is NOW, then that is the only element of proof you need. You are ready. No other reasoning applies. You are ready! So you must act. NOW!!

■■■■■■■■■■■■■■■■■■■■■■■■■■■■■■■■■■■■■■■■■■■■■

# April 1

*The morning after is always uncomfortable when you go to bed with a want and wake up beside a need. –ali–*

The classic agreement is that there is no right or wrong time to get involved in your own development. The essential thing is to stay involved because it is this tenacity that will personally acquaint you with your most enabling and enduring qualities. Recall that there is absolutely never any reason, plausible or otherwise, to wait on the right life-cycle, whether biorhythm or menstrual, before you get lost in finding yourself. Naturally, most people desire to improve themselves, but they focus their attention on external things as if *"bigger"*, *"better"* *"more"* are the proper incubators of success. Instead they should concentrate on the internal *"wants"* that fuel such desires because once you understand how to shrink the value of your wants, you will maintain more energy to satisfy your needs. And that is the key to individualized wealth-building. Needs need satisfying. Wants can wait.

## April 2

*Having nothing to lose is like having no food to eat, and hunger is the greatest pain of all.  –ali-*

When it comes to "getting-it-together",  you merely cannabilize a part of yourself if you seek to soar on the painless route.  That is simply an experiment with the notion that you have nothing to lose. You do. Once you begin the search for self-improvement, you must forfeit participation in the commonplace  "adventure"  of standing still.  You must build up a reputation as a champion of moving forward. This sets the stage for what is called ***"activity analysis"*** where you structure your time so that nothing of value will be diminished by what you do to and for yourself.  How do you do this? By patiently monitoring situations and developing skills that will  allow you to target those numerous, unspecified situations that will be good for you. Remember that when  using your time wisely becomes a preferred project, it prevents you from intruding into the eye-catching glitter of  *"doing something to keep from  doing nothing" syndrome.* And that's like showing favoritism to foolishness.

# April 3

*Tears are the 1<sup>st</sup> seeds of power.* *—ali—*

Don't become discouraged if you find it difficult to renegotiate terms with yourself. This is what happens when you are too familiar with the reluctance to exert more control over your affairs. You have a "stand-still agreement" with success. Much of this stems from your anticipatory level. *You want nothing!!* You must re-shift your focus and though it will take a number of steps to increase your confidence in yourself, first of all, you must move away from the wait-and-see attitude which restricts your attention to yourself and permits you to feel that you lack the skills to deal with your situation. That is learning the hard way. There's a more reasonable way to come to terms with you. Stop haunting yourself with the illegitimate power of not knowing what to do to get what you want. Ever since the day you were born and crying became the "platinum card" to getting your demands met, you came into your own. However, now you must take this "birthright" and refine it because it is still the standard by which you will make your demands known. Only now, the basic science of crying must be upgraded. As you grow older, the dynamics change from crying to trying. That's the secret. Don't cry---try!

## April 4

*Progress is the cry of success.   −ali−*

The natural law that compels others to do your bidding is etched in the small independent power of a baby's tears. This is your very 1$^{st}$ contact with the success of gaining attention to your needs, but most individuals never learn to convey or translate the language of tears into a more acceptable mode of operation  once they mature. And that's a pity since you must always use what you've got to get what you want. Remember that the best way 2 go from crying 2 trying is learning to apply yourself!

## April 5

*If you are a fool, then what you expect out of life can adversely affect your life expectancy.   _ali-*

At some point, you will need to find compromise between your life expectancy and what you expect out of life. When you reach the point where both are compatible, then you balance all your speculations so that you can become the beneficiary of them.

## April 6

*No situation is so dire that you should restrict your attention to yourself and feel that that you don't possess the skills to deal with it.*
*--ali-*

You have many strengths. 1$^{st}$ of all, you have a firm relationship with your point of distinction. Accessorize this strength, whatever it is, and it becomes an added bonus. If you can do something well, no one can thwart your efforts to be interested in your own talents. Timely interests in your own talents not only reduces your response to despair, it also provides you with the ability to save yourself. You jump ahead of insecurity by self-reliability, and nothing lasts longer than trust in your own skills. The goal is to make yourself popular with yourself. Once this is accomplished, your life will behave better.

## April 7

### *Ponder all things*

Ponder all options. What's at stake is your ability not to be overwhelmed by the payback of not being focused. When you are trying to gain self-approval, don't promise yourself the future if you have a record of not being able to finish what you have started. Get Help! And all you really need to do is to lose track of your appeal for placing yourself at a disadvantage. Just by doing this, you preserve choices. And this is particularly useful because it frees you from unnecessary stress and allows you to approach real problems with complete detachment from distraction. The whole premise is to never underestimate the plausibility of how perfectly you can deal with your own imperfections. The reason: you have a strong tendency to always treat yourself better than deserved.

## April 8

*You plan a good deed whenever you plant a good seed. –ali-*

Plant a seed. Everything will be coming up roses once you stop moonlighting with only a partial interest in your right to dream. Know that your most dramatic growth will take place when you unravel the mystery of how not to hold on to dreams that you should let go of.

## April 9

*Being totally absorbed in the "blues" is like playing hookey from life.   –ali–*

Now is the politically correct moment to cease stumbling over the leftover vestiges of "somebody-done-you-wrong". This is the peripheral consent to remain poised on the whipping-post end of change where your life will always dip precariously into the chasm of you feeling sorry for you. The "blues" obstruct your need to be intelligently critical and impedes your ability to recognize when "enuff is enuff". More precisely, the "blues" gobble up your impact to be functionally encouraging too yourself. In the battle to win back your confidence , your self-esteem can sometimes get lost in the gut-wrenching cycle of depression, and  whenever your will to live is being mentally auctioned off, then you are testing your limits to self-destruct. And that's not the smartest thing to do.

## April 10

*To cure yourself, 1$^{st}$ you have to care 4 yourself.* — ali-

The smart thing to do is this: stop spending enormous amounts of energy and time that produces only a rippling effect with the affairs of your life. Show more optimism for yourself. Explode. Become your own godsend. How?! By establishing a network of growth that opens the door to improving the spectrum of everything you do. In the absence of crystal clear data that going "bust" in life is the divine plan for you, engage in behavior that not only ensures day-to-day well-being, but also treats and corrects anything that makes you fall short of permanent emotional stability. How is it done? By simply shifting your focus from how to *cure* your life to how to <u>*care*</u> for your life. To cure and treat yourself you must be stoic and remote, impassively distant. But to care for yourself is different. Caring permits you to get closer to the **"what-is-really-going-on"** with you, and this proximity grants you a mental framework for a quicker response. By the way, the cure is 2 care.

## April 11

*The phenomenon is not to protect yourself from life*
*but to protect your life from yourself.* –ali–

Taken to its logical extreme, success ultimately depends on your belief that you deserve a life more reliable than a do-it-yourself, day-to-day routine that is subject to the whims of fate. There is no drum roll for you if you recoil at any suggestions that you are not bound by limitations. As long as you breathe and exist without seeing any positive changes in your short-term outlook, then your life is affected with not enough flexibility to relate to your own needs. When this happens, your thumbnail sketch of yourself allows you to experience the phenomenon of temporary insanity because at any point where your desire to improve falls to inappropriate levels, you are slumping towards rock-bottom. When you develop a high tolerance for the cheap thrill of fooling yourself, you will face a combination of things. (1) As a fool, you become attractive to those who can spot a sucka, (2) You will be scared away from helping yourself because the best possible advice you can give yourself is meaningless, (3) You misunderstand how much of living is lost by attempting to protect yourself from life than from protecting your life from yourself!

# April 12

*No man has ever beat the odds of making it to # 1 without 1$^{st}$ knowing exactly what was going on in his life. —ali-*

What's happening at any given moment in your life is personally significant. Knowing this is part of the link between being either hostile or helpful too yourself. Both require a huge amount of energy to sustain themselves, but only one is healthy in the long run. Think Fast!

## April 13

*Rumor has it that until you liberate yourself from other people's opinion, you will continue to act like a rat in a maze. —ali—*

When you consciously admire the rumors that friends inherit from your past failures, you learn how to intellectually symbolize your accomplishments so that what you do is less a personal matter and more about proving 'em wrong. This type of allure raises a veil of invisibility over your specific ability to shape your behavior for the better because when you are committed to the insights of others, you lack the necessary tools to work as hard as possible in your own behalf since the challenges you face will not be tied to your own motivations. They, instead, will be diversions on lease.

## April 14

*Men are the commodity that money monopolizes.* —
*ali-*

If you think the catalyst for your success is going to be the residual crumbs of someone else's largesse---you're wrong as hell. And to minimize confusion, here's why. **Men are a monopoly that money dominates!**

## April 15

*The secret is out.  Once you start kissing feet, asses are next.  —ali-*

It's no secret.    The epitome of servile convenience is to be mentally accessible to kiss the feet of those you don't wish to offend  Who you rely on oftentimes coincides with your standards and ideals about values.  This depersonalization of yourself allows you to transform your independence into dependency  Remember that when you rely on others beyond permissible limits, you place vital  information about yourself into hands where it doesn't belong, and this invites them to invade your privacy. Please recognize that when your actions inform another of your dependency, then your dependency is always subject to use that leads straight to you being *used.*

## April 16

*Have sympathy for the devil.   He is always close by when you madly build your life around things you enjoy ,but he goes on vacation when your life is restrained out of respect for the things you fear.  – ali-*

Every life comes equipped with a self-regulating preference to fluctuate wildly, and while there is no simple procedure to detect or delete this flaw, you are not obligated to function improperly or insanely. The real damage occurs from the not-so-anonymous process of not providing yourself with a more predictable lifestyle.   Douse the flames of this best bet for disaster. It is pivotal that it not serve full-term because the only way it can satisfy itself is to devour the shelf life of your incentive to excel. Don't permit your own demons to pare down the quality of your life.

## April 17

*Success is the divine acknowledgment that God placed you exactly where you needed to be to make the best use of what He gave you to get what you want. –ali-*

Once you invent the concept of making yourself a productive human being, you award yourself with content by never turning back. Recall this reminder. Any reverse changes that result from you not being prepared or simply being caught off guard is not a new challenge. It is an impulse to flirt with disaster. And it's also a sign of what will happen in the future because it's the price tag of not having an agenda you can bet your ass on. Another piece of advice to recall is that the major obstacle to establishing a winning attitude is that so many individuals search for odd and/or novel ways to provide a safe haven for their goals that they fail to realize that simplicity is the best idea. Unfortunately, the benefits of simplicity is diminished by the preferential treatment we give to the notion that there is no "gain without pain". So many time this is dead wrong, so don't feed your appetite for self-destruction. Go on a diet today!

## April 18.

*Ignorance is not good news.* –ali-

Any time you are unfamiliar with being right, the ignorance of the "good news" "no-one-knows-for-sure" syndrome is what occurs. Willingly working with this presumption is a personal admission of wrongdoing against your better judgment. Additionally, one of the most vexing problems with this line of thinking lies in its maintenance. Since no one knows what to do, no one is there to service your breakdown. You must get back to the simplistic reality of addressing both your current and future needs by the evolving nature of your right to use what you've got to get what you want. And do you know what you've got: **the divine acknowledgment that God placed you where you needed to be to make the best use of your talent.**

## April 19

*Failure inflames self-hatred.  –ali–*

You can triumph!  When you are unwilling to accept this self-fulfilling personal prophecy, you harbor a dehabilitating bias against yourself that is at total odds with the image and emergence of individual success.  This disbelief strips away much of your inner strength and supports the reality that *your success can only arise out of a situation whose reality was not invented by you.*  By estimating the chances of your success based upon faulty internal information, you run the risk of establishing guarantees that your personal integrity is constrained by this underestimation of yourself. Don't embrace the fire of this unrealistic assumption. Otherwise, you double your capacity to fall short, but even without  this increase in dumbing yourself down, you influence yourself to over-react when you are sanctioned by your flaws, and this only enlarges the speculative appeal of the wrong choice of not believing in yourself. You can triumph!

# April 20

*Your insecurities are the lynch mob that will hang*
*you by the scruff of your soul. –ali–*

Feeding on your own insecurity is a predatory act that allows you to verify your own self-destruction. By deviating from the law of self-conservation, you critically weaken your chances of success by not exploring ways to improve yourself. Be advised that passive intervention is no prevention, and that your clutching-at-straws desperation bears little resemblance to your actual survival quotient. You must recognize that although you have provided yourself the lifetime job of feeling sorry for yourself, it will become too mentally expensive to justify. Here's the point. Insecurity invests you with a lynch mob mentality towards yourself whose principle weapon is the arrogance of ignorance. What you must recall is that ignorance will go to great lengths to make you a perfect fit for foolish behavior. Your ultimate burden then will be to expand old ideas of failure into new possibilities. Otherwise,you are no longer essential.

# SNAPSHOTS

## April 21

*Don't fluctuate. Elevate.  —ali-*

Remember that severe, unpredictable fluctuations in your life indicate that you don't trust yourself enough to specify your priorities. And this ensures that for the most part, feedback from your actions will be negative or at best, critically deficient, and given the enormous potential of our human capabilities, this is like placing your goals in escrow. Even though stress, taxes, war, and death will never completely allow our lives to totally function under normal operating conditions at all times, you can slow down the moody fluctuations by permitting your time to be served in accordance with the specifications of its own restraints! How it's done?  Try this.  Instead of building your existence to maximize the getting-of-the-things-you-like, construct it to minimize the contact of the things you fear.

## April 22

*For the uninformed, living and breathing at the same time is a concert where they don't know when to applaud. –ali-*

Dig this. You must live out loud. This is the primary reason for your independence and the character of you being unique. Your individuality opens the door for you to close the door so that no one will step through to discourage you from ever being in short supply of personal optimism. You must shine for you. Living out loud is the higher-than-expected characterization of each day becoming life well-lived. Conventional wisdom suggests that if you are mystified by the act of being and breathing at the same time, then you serve no purpose. You are simply the downside of who you should be.

## April 23

*To understand who you are requires the knowledge
of accepting what you are.  —ali-*

Lacking intimate contact with yourself always increases the possibility that you will end up keeping up with the  many ways of selling yourself short.  That much is certain.  Why?  Because you cannot budget ignorance!  When you adapt to the changing landscape of ignorance without a sense of knowing that you are simply a well-heeled patron of your own inner darkness, you are merely accumulating credit as your own personal special-kind-of-fool.

## April 24

*Go. Grow. Glow.*

If, for whatever reason, you feel you can attempt developmental growth without investing in a new attitude towards yourself, then you should refrain from making predictions about how great your life is going to become. Chances are that it won't change much because as a general rule, "life predictions" are accessible only to those capable of understanding that being slow, stubborn, or stupid will not make life any easier. Remember that since there is no reasonable alternative to decisions and choices, why not make them intelligently?

## April 25

*Unplug. Sing in the key of YOU. Dance to your own drum. —ali-*

Unplug. To live out loud you must  step out of the shadows where your life is plugged into the "ordinary" because on average, being average makes you a zero. Being content with either "average" or "ordinary" proves a pretty good estimate of how meaningless you imagine yourself to be. If you have determined that "average" and "ordinary" are the way to go for you , then you have not really done a good job of  evaluating your individual value. And that's a sad commentary on how extraordinarily good you have become at being ordinarily average.

## April 26

*Never raise the bar at the bar.  –ali–*

Don't be afraid to raise the bar because by reasonably pushing yourself beyond your self-imposed limits, you  inspire yourself to greater confidence in your  belief in you.. But why not take it one step further. Rather than making a "bid on opportunities" that come your way,  seize them. Does that sound hard to do? Not if you honestly believe in rewarding yourself for the simple pleasure of being alive. Nothing is impossible once you come to accept that every precious breath you take should never be exchanged except for something that will make the next breath even more enjoyable and worthwhile.

## April 27

*Coming of age before you age has its privileges.* —
*ali-*

It should come as no surprise to you that in exchange for the privilege of being and breathing that something is expected of you. And it's your contribution to making the world a better place. You do this by *becoming.* And if you are one of those people who just don't get it.........understand this. You become not by trading your energy back and forth between the seconds, the minutes, the hours that make up each day. You become by using your time to make use of your potential to be better. And that's the real deal.

## April 28

*A lie you tell yourself and then make yourself*
*believe is the risky behavior that makes you a fool.*
*−ali−*

Your behavior towards yourself is not etched in stone. This means you possess the ability to short-circuit any abnormal acts you may wish to commit against yourself. Lying to yourself is one such act. Rather than blindly leading yourself to believe that a good lie to yourself is a strategy to head off disappointment or despair, end this risky behavior. A lie is nothing more than an investment in short-term thinking. You must seek the *Big Picture*. Throw away the notion that a lie is a magic formula. It's not. Neither is it an exclamation point to showcase how brilliant you are at just getting by for another day on "mismanaged" time. Instead, a lie, not matter how cleverly invented , is the period at the end of the death sentence you award yourself when you under-price the value of being smart enough to devise a workable strategy to improve your life. But there's more. Once you cease to make guesses and estimates, and start to traffic in facts, then you will realize just how cheap a lie is. And how dangerous.

## April 29

*When you diminish yourself, you finish yourself.*
*—ali—*

What is necessarily so is that all your interactions with your environment should work towards making you "master of the domain". None of your actions should ever diminish your efforts to forge ahead or to stay out of harm's way. You must mandate change in your life, partly for the reason that there is too much going on for you to miss out on. Going through life diminished by roadblocks and handicaps only proves your faithlessness in the concept that life is meant to be enjoyed to its fullest. Stop building your own prison out of the bricks of your not knowing or caring enough about yourself to provide better for yourself. The solution is not just to look ahead, but to look ahead with a solution. Primarily, your "misery index" is often a good indicator of what is wrong in your life since it gives you a fair estimate of what you need to eliminate from your life. Then you take your head out of the sand.

## April 30

*Panic and pain are the twins symbols of waiting 2
long 2 take action.*
*-ali-*

The short answer is this: Never panic!

## May 1

*Vision is the power to feel your way through the darkness with your eyes closed.   –ali-*

A last minute dash to the finish line cannot guarantee success. You must have vision. Vision allows you to start the race before you even get there and due to the increasing complexities and challenges ushered in by technology, vision as a resource is very important. More intense competition in the marketplace has escalated, changing the mode and scale by which business is conducted which makes it even more vital that you be able to see ahead of your footsteps. Clear vision will permit you to diverge from the pack and blaze new paths out of the long-standing traditions that govern the workplace. You will not be hemmed in and you will be able to anticipate any revolutionary change that you did not, in fact, initiate. Vision requires making far-reaching  concessions to your belief in yourself.  It also means destroying any built-in limits you may entertain about the substance of your dreams because vision is the principal power that not only permits you to protect the integrity of your dreams, but allows you a front row seat in making much needed decisions before they reach critical mass.  To succeed, you have to be able to see. Clearly.

## May 2

*Vision is hindsight going in the opposite direction. —ali-*

Everyone on the planet has 20/20 hindsight. Everything is so crystal clear after the fact that you are usually stunned that you didn't see it, notice it, or do it earlier. Most often this startling clarity comes into focus only after you've been unceremoniously declared a loser. That's what hindsight is---corrective lens for chumps. On the other hand, vision is the legacy of seeing the end of things before the beginning, a personalized snapshot of history waiting to happen. If you can't see far enough ahead of your dreams, the bogeyman will get you and your cherished goals will fade to gray, becoming a nightmare. You must be able to see in order to predict outcomes and this is, in sum, what success entails: being able to predict outcomes in advance of their maturity. Vision equals the ability to PLAN, to PREDICT, to PROGRESS.

## May 3

*Don't make travel plans until you have packed your vision......-ali-*

Vision is the working contract between your plans and the hard work needed to guarantee success, but how does the process work? Plans are the poetic, swanlike, graceful embodiment of a goal. On paper and in theory, they leap and soar with majesty, quickening the heart and stirring the blood. Plans are delicate, a joy to behold: ballet dancers. But how do you make them get their hands dirty? Vision. Vision is what converts plans into hard work, giving them the support they need to emerge from paper into iron. Plans unattended to by hard work can never expand from their small base until they are connected to your vision which is the frequent flier between what is now and what you know can be. The process loosely is this. (1) You perceive a vision (inert action): (2) you formulate a plan (action); (3) you employ hard work (effective action). So in essence, action is the kick-in-the-ass that powers you through the process. Get busy!
■■■■■■■■■■■■■■■■■■■■■■■■■■■■■■■■■■■■■■■■■■■■

May 4$^{th}$

*Success leaves no leftovers.*
-ali-

When you recognize who you are, lesser evolved men will do your bidding.
Fools are but the conveniences of any who desire to use them. This is not Sesame Street. This is not Mayberry. And this is not Mr. Roger's neighborhood. This is life, the hard, cold turf of mortal men who must clash and scramble and wage war for the goods of the earth. There is no stop sign, no red light that force us to share or be humane. This is the real deal where men lose on a daily basis, so get real. Ain't nuthin' left over after success but heartache and pain. Choose your weapons. Know who you are, what you want and then rattle your sword. Take today and enslave it. Make it work for you or at least against other men. This ain't no disco. This is life and you're in the trenches.

## May 5

## GO NOW!

Start immediately. If you desire to quit smoking, don't delay your journey until you're finished the pack you're smoking. Crush the pack and start now. Don't wait until after supper to begin your diet. Consider it officially on right now. Our fear of failure and what it could do to our self-esteem is what holds us back, so we procrastinate, waiting on a sign. We pray that maybe tomorrow, we'll have the fortitude to signal ourselves to go. **Go now**. There is no sure way to know if waiting will serve any useful purpose, but you do know waiting will keep you enslaved longer. **Go now**. Delay is nothing more than the premium between your fear and your delight in bondage. **Go now**. The rewards significantly outweigh the risks. If you fail, you're simply what you always were----a slave. But what if you succeed? Delay locks you into defeat, permanent enrollment in the imperiled environment of your doomed mental outlook. **Go now**. Even though stepping out does not always necessarily mean breaking free, it is always a prelude to standing up and facing your slavish behavior. **Go now**.

## May 6<sup>th</sup>

*How can you eliminate the fear of shooting yourself when you don't even know what it is that makes the gun dangerous?*
-Ali-

At its least coercive, fear is the nuts and bolts of a contract on yourself. Fear is the proverbial gun with which you shoot yourself in the foot anytime you pull it out to play with it. Fear will never award you the liberty to solicit meaningful outside help because you lack the will to ask pertinent questions. As such you belong to the network of fools who shop for clouds without silver linings. Cancel your fear eligibility. How? By loving someone else enough to do it for them! Since your self-esteem is a walled fortress of your hatred for yourself, it may still permit you to love someone else. If you can't muster enough love for yourself to fix what's wrong in your life, then try your love on someone else for size. Just maybe, you'll be able to fool fear. Love is all you need.

## May 7

*The quality of life is not a commitment to making it through a losing today, but with stringing together a whole lot of winning tomorrows. —ali-*

For the next few minutes, take a quick look at your life and examine its conditions. If it is really that disorganized, you can always return later, but do it. This is a private assessment so there is no need to publicize your findings. If your life is robust and healthy, then without delay you should pray for you indeed are a blessed child. On the other hand, if you discover that you are depressed, lonely, confined, a smoker, physically inactive, eating unhealthy, or not maintaining your optimal weight, then you must accept these discoveries as receipts of notice that you are a self-molester. You take advantage of yourself. You pick on yourself. You may exercise no control over public policy ,but you have control over your personal agenda, and when you encourage yourself to smoke, drink and eat unwisely then you mirror the desires of government and big business by heaping contempt upon yourself. You grant yourself permission for this abuse. Just say NO!

*May 8*

*Health should not be used as a down payment*
*for wealth.*
*-ali-*

This country eats its young. And no part of your life is not affected or influenced by this feeding frenzy. Consider this. The government has shown that it doesn't support good health by slashing the budget of Medicare programs. Big biz'ness has likewise flaunted its disregard for good health by promoting unhealthy lifestyles (by advertising and selling alcohol and nicotine etc) but most frightening is the fact that doctors do not support good health. In a survey this year, it was found that most doctors fail to counsel patients about healthful behavior! Shocking, especially when that should be an integral part of their function. Yet, their perception is that they don't feel they have much impact on patient behavior so they don't provide you with a lot of life-saving advice. But what can you do when the lure of an unhealthy lifestyle is so appealing? Since you must realize that you can expect nothing from others, you must expect everything from yourself. Fight for your health. The same attitude you exhibit toward your wealth concerns should be the same one you exhibit towards your health concerns. It's all in your head. And in your hands.

# May 9

## *Aging is a voucher for dying    -ali-*

As you contemplate future success, don't forget to pencil in aging. If you have a 10 year plan, you must also take note of the fact that you will be a decade older and your health may be tremendously different then, so you have to chart a parallel course to maintain a reasonable level of fitness and health. To enjoy life fully, being fiscally fit is only a facet of the equation. You must be aggressive in your attempt to be physically fit also. In the same way that it is unwise to attempt negotiating the future with an outdated frame of reference, it is also important that our projections for the future be honest assessments of our health forecast. Right now, as we analyze our future, we broadcast the picture of ourselves as is, but will that actually be the real you then? I will never forget the day when Nelson Mandela was released from prison after 27 years of confinement. I was momentarily stunned when I saw him. He was Nelson Mandela alright, but not the man of all the photos I had seen. There had been no recent photos of him so I had forgot to add 27 years to the picture I had of him in my mind. I was expecting Mandela the boxer. It was then that I was amazed at how easy it is to project ourselves through the future without showing any signs of aging. To understand our future strength, we must realize the value of good health and then take steps to maintaining it. There can be no true success if it is gained at the expense of your health. . You must plan for health as you plan for wealth.
■■■■■■■■■■■■■■■■■■■■■■■■■■■■■■■■■■■■■■■■■■

# May 10

*Get a pre-nup! When the honeymoon with wealth is over and you find that your health is failing, then rest assured that the bitch has robbed you blind.*
*–ali-*

Any get rich scheme that does not award you a program of health as part of its package is virtually a scam unless it promises the riches quickly. If the program has to develop over a number of years then health warnings should be affixed. In order to be a truly satisfied customer, your health as well as your wealth must be considered. Are you laughing yet? Well don't. I know many of you will never permit yourselves to indulge in the whimsy of any of those get-rich-quick schemes that are advertised in books, magazines and newspapers. They're amusing, aren't they? But what is a career? Technically, it's a get rich scheme. Jobs make ends meet. A profession makes you rich, so when you bounce into bed with one, look hard into her eyes the morning after. No matter how beautiful she was when you got into bed, chances are she is less desirable with the makeup off. Be prepared. In the dark, they all look alike, so train yourself to become devoted to satisfying your own needs (when it comes to health). Don't live vicariously. Live victoriously. Plan to be healthy. Don't misunderstand how important health concerns are to any plans you make for success. You could die without them.

# May 11

*In a good success plan, purpose is like elbow grease that keeps everything going, while performance merely keeps you upright. Don't get them twisted or you won't know your ass from your elbow.     –ali–*

A good success plan should define your purpose and not simply measure your performance. This is important because performance can become symbolic and erupt into a ceremony for patting yourself on the back while your purpose has gotten lost in the smugness of "getting there". To avoid this, always remember to adjust your purpose for success to complement your performance because many people reach their goals with their sense of purpose missing. It's easy to do because in personal development, the attention is on performance which usually has a much higher, more visible external context. Performance is also more competitive and can bear the scrutiny of comparison with someone else's achievements or failures. Purpose is more of an introvert, personal. It is the intimate, private reason for your desire to succeed and it rarely gets applauded by others as you near your goal. As you start to fit into smaller and smaller dress sizes, your friends commend and congratulate your performance while never realizing that your purpose for losing weight was to set an example for you mother. In acknowledging the hoopla of the back-slapping, the true purpose of your mission is lost. . It's easy to let performance alone become the yardstick for success when it is purpose that keeps you centered and focused. Many people surrender their purpose... That's why they appear conceited. Don't let that happen to you. Put a smile on your purpose and miles on your performance.
■■■■■■■■■■■■■■■■■■■■■■■■■■■■■■■■■■■■■■

## May 12

*If you lack planning, then save the world the example of another failure. Cop out now so no one will have to buy you out so you can sell out.*
*–ali–*

# May 13

*In a society where anything goes, sex is the X
that marks the spot.   –ali–*

Vision. Purpose. Extreme notions that over the last few decades have almost gotten smothered under layers of techno-dollars where money has created the whole new industry of "anything goes". When the purpose of the entertainment industry changed, human behavior was modified to serve the needs of this change. We simply maximized our shock quotient to accept the corresponding loss of our morals. The purpose of the industry initially was merely to provide entertainment, but when huge profits divided the various segments of the industry up into "us-versus them", men had to create methods to gain an advantage over the competition.  It was then that purpose veered clear of entertainment for arts' sake. It was then that sex became the focal point. Consequently, a whole new marketing strategy evolved to support the selling of sex. So, never underestimate the power of purpose. It was so powerful that it was able to shake loose the moral foundation of this Christian country and to prevail against the teachings of the Bible until sex and violence are as common as the 10 Commandments. Now that you recognize power when you see it, embrace it and use it to your advantage. Purpose is industrial strength, but it will work for you. Choose it and use it.

■■■■■■■■■■■■■■■■■■■■■■■■■■■■■■■■■■■■■■■■■

# May 14

*Practice does not make perfect because to practice the wrong thing over and over and over again is a "Go directly to fail" card.  –ali-*

Do your goals and dreams have a high turnover rate? Once you pass go, do you find it difficult to retain the energy or initiative to aggressively give pursuit to what you set out to do? If so, you are threatened by a lack of discipline. Didn't anyone tell you that discipline is like a set of training wheels which will keep you moving when you want to give up on yourself? It is the proof of the pudding that separates the winners from the losers. It is the simple idea of doing it over and over and over again so that it remains perfect. When someone tells you that practice makes perfect, thank them but don't entirely heed them because they have given you a "go directly to fail" card. Practice does not make perfect. Only *perfect* practice makes perfect! You can practice a technique a 1000 times but if your execution is wrong, mere repetition will not correct it. To be perfect, you must practice the technique correctly. Nowhere is this more evident than in martial arts, but it aptly applies to everything. To succeed, you must possess the discipline to stick with your goals. It may mean getting up early each day to shoot free throws, but it gives you the confidence needed to stay in touch with your dreams. There's no reason to scatter-dance from one dream to another as if none of them are functional. They're probably in fine working order. It's just that your technique is wrong. Go get your training wheels!

## May 15

*This is a power grab. Let's review this month's ½ menu.*

*You cannot run the race of life*
*If your dream is crippled by fear*
*How fast, how far do you expect to get*
*If your vision is not crystal clear.*
*Why delay the doing of what you've got to do*
*When your wealth and health are failing*
*Procrastination will chew you up and spit you out*
*And you won't even know you were ailing.*
*A good success plan is all that you need*
*Where your purpose and performance may speak;*
*A mission where your discipline rules*
*And separates you from the weak.*
*Don't trade your hope for a pot of fool's gold*
*And don't slow down your pace*
*For with vision and purpose before you*
*You're bound to win the race.*

## *May 16*

*Write your life in bold colors. Don't die without living.   –ali–*

The single, most important lesson to learn is that you are alone. Included in this is the classic truth: You alone are responsible for your success. Absorb that. And in this way you can dodge the network of fools who think the world owes them something 'cause there're here. This is very self-destructive thinking.  You are here. There are no rewards for your conception. End of story. If you so choose,  you can fill the blanks pages between your birth and death with the invisible ink of mediocrity or you can write boldly by taking what you want. To thrive is to punctuate your life with boldness and flair. You must slow the fast-spinning world down and make it offer you its services. Don't be a wallflower at the dance of existence. You won't get a return match with life so the time is now to direct the traffic of your comings and goings. Be not timid.  You may be alone but only you know what you want and that is a good enough reason to get it. You exist so it belongs to you. 'Nuff said

## May 17

*Be YOU------**BOLDLY!***

Today I will stare down the corridor of dawn and demand that the sun shine brightest on me. I know who I am therefore I am most worthy. I will stand naked beneath the canopy of the heavens and demand that today's 24 hours work in my behalf, awarding me time enough to count my blessings and to stay 2 steps ahead of the rest of the world. Today, I will be what I was born to be----ME----and in the wake of my becoming King, smaller men will build my kingdom!

■■■■■■■■■■■■■■■■■■■■■■■■■■■■■■■■■■■■■■■

# May 18

*Success leaves no leftovers.   —ali-*

When you recognize who you are. Lesser evolved men will do your bidding. Fools are but the conveniences of any who desire to use them... This is not Sesame Street. This is not Mayberry. And this is not Mr. Rogers's neighborhood. This is life; the hard, cold turf of mortal men who must clash and compete for the goods of the earth. There is no stop sign, no red light that forces us to share or to be humane. This is the real deal where men lose on a daily basis, so get out your battle ax. Ain't nuthin' left over after success but heartache and pain. Choose your weapons carefully. Know who you are, what you want and then rattle your sword. Take today and enslave it. Make it work for you or at least against other men. This ain't no disco. This is life during wartime and your ass is in the trenches.

■■■■■■■■■■■■■■■■■■■■■■■■■■■■■■■■■■■■■■■■■

## May 19

*Whenever you're doing it with yourself, make
sure the curtains are closed.   –ali-*

Life is a relatively short term affair that
carries its own dangers and too often, we
intensify the popularity of these risks by our
voracious appetite to perform unnatural acts
with ourselves. Deliberately cloning yourself in
the image of an idol or role model is a type of
psychological incest that to some great extent
destroys your potential for future natural
development. It couldn't be any worse if you let
that person rule your life, laying plans for every
move you make.   Sounds a lot like prison,
doesn't it? That's where a whole lot of Superfly
and Scarface copycats are right now. Prison.  At
least they recognize their chains. It is never and
can never be exciting living in isolation of the
person God intended you to be. How can you
receive your blessings when you're walking in
someone else's shoes? You're too far away
from home to catch the bus. Have patience with
yourself. There is someone waiting----------
YOU
■■■■■■■■■■■■■■■■■■■■■■■■■■■■■■■■■■■■

## May 20

*Good health is wealth's shot in the arm.  –ali-*

Despite all the kudos applauding the recent medical breakthroughs, no more than a wink has gone towards the study of the planet beneath the skin. This is real estate worth examining, especially if we, as humans, are to live productive lives. When we come to understand the chemistry of man's mind or the biology of his soul then maybe we can pinpoint the reasons why man kills with such wanton abandon or why he destroys the earth upon which he lives. Man's ignorance of himself is so great that his love for self and kind has evaporated or gone up in the smoke of his misguided altruism. He would rather "save the whales" than "save the males"; adopt a highway than adopt a child. Even worse, this same man will lovingly build a comfortable house for his dog and then put his own parents in a nursing home. He will donate endless energy to his favorite charity and then lack the time to read his child a bedtime story. It is not the cancer of man's body that is so aggravating, but the cancer of his soul.  If no cure is soon found, we may not celebrate another millennium

# May 21

*When you know you're special, specialize in it.   –ali–*

Here's food for thought. If you want to know how important you are to God, just turn on your television or your radio. See that......hear that? Those actresses, actors and
athletes that you see on the screen; the singers, musicians, and rappers that you hear on the radio are the best. The crème de la crème. Not only because they have spent countless years studying their craft and honing their skills, but more so because God thought so much of you. In all things, he wants only the best for you so he didn't make it easy to become a star, and this shows how important you are. Think about this. Even as babies, you always bought your children  the biggest and the brightest rattler for their entertainment because they were special to you. Only the best for them, and that's what God has done for you with the Cam Newtons, Michael Jacksons, and Beyonces of the world. He wanted them to entertain you! You were provided with such a luminous cast of stars, not so you could emulate them, but so they could entertain you! The Creator knew that after a long day on the road to find yourself that you would need to relax, so he provided you with the best crop of entertainers the world has ever known. Now, ain't that loving you? Whenever you recognize the wonderful talents of these gifted individuals that should speed you on to self-actualization, so you can fulfill your own potential. Be ye a writer, a teacher, a doctor, come on with it. Others wait to be entertained by your skills. The next time you see one of your heroes perform; just remember how important you truly are.

## May 22
*Go.  You never have to worry about where the
gravy train is stopping.        —ali-*

GO. But remember this. At any time when you exercise the right to move forward, you must also invent the responsibility to keep moving.  Standing still or moving backwards does not have the same effect and neither of these options will permit you to transcend the tendency to manufacture illusory gains where, in effect, none exist.   What these conditions allow you to experience is the world moving past you rather than you moving past the world. Moving forward, at any pace, allows you the mobility to migrate from standard to improved conditions based merely on the *returns of transition.*   This means you can levy service from information and skills you now possess and instantly benefit with their transfer to a new dimension (place). For instance when McDonalds took its show on the road to Japan, it found a niche after the novelty grew thin by offering fare comparable with Japanese food taste. Ronald McDonald understands the *returns of transition* and this is why in places such as LA, the fare is inspired by regional appeal. However, the *returns of transition* are not limited to that example. It is applicable across the board. Even on a personal level. It is merely a bonus for you being bold enough to move forward. When you work your diet and results start popping out.   Those compliments and appreciative stares. Know what they are?   That's right. They are the *returns of transitions* awarding you your well-deserved bonus for stepping up and moving forward. Quit smoking and the saved money. Guess what it will be? You got that right. I don't have to tell you. Go. And keep moving. It's called riding the gravy train...

## May 23

*A choice should be a nomination for growth and advancement. –ali–*

The whole idea of advancement is to eliminate any reason you may have for standing still. The rise and fall of choice is never a plausible excuse to stand still because contained within the very dynamics of every choice is the seed of growth. Choice induces development. That is their nature and the whole bargain of decision-making rests upon the intrinsic value of choice never leaving you worst off than before. Remember this. A real choice, whether a low demand one or a high demand one, is a nomination for advancement. You either benefit or you should lose nothing, remaining as is. Now, don't forget this. A choice becomes a gamble only when the mutual weight of its consequences and the menace of its possibilities acquaint you with a decision between the lesser of 2 evils! This is a gamble----not a choice. Don't get them twisted. Or they will leave you dazed and confused.
∎∎∎∎∎∎∎∎∎∎∎∎∎∎∎∎∎∎∎∎∎∎∎∎∎∎∎∎∎∎∎∎∎∎∎∎∎

## May 24

*A gamble is a choice in a pressure cooker.  —
ali-*

Once you are able to clearly distinguish the characteristics that separate a choice from a gamble, you will be more willing to move forward and to unlock the next level of your experience.  Once the penalty phase is removed from what you assume are choices, you will become much more confident in advancing yourself.  Choose and move. Don't get trampled by a gamble. Choices and gambles are both psychic motifs that labor under a contingency fee and the operant that blurs the line between them is stress. Minus stress, everything is in sharper focus and a gamble is hardly worth a second glance, but stress coming into bud allows us to become unimpressed or disillusioned by the real choices available, forcing us to seek something more exotic. That's when we cross the line and gamble. Choices are simple, plain Janes in granny dresses. Gambles are exotic dancers in g-strings. Recognize them when you see them, but remember this:  when they're naked they both look alike. Don't be fooled. One goes up. One goes down. And stress is the tattoo that distinguishes them. Hello.

## May 25

*At least know why you're ignorant.    –ali-*

Ignorance is not bliss, and a move between the lesser of 2 evils is not a choice... Such thoughtlessness will get you reprimanded by reality. Bear this in mind. The greatest function of reality is to keep the big picture clear at all times and under all circumstances, so whenever anything else claims the right to adjust the clarity of your big picture, rest assured that the resolution will dim. And in this age of mass technology, the enormous emotional ambivalence of deciding between the lesser of 2 evils is a no-win situation for you. One just postpones defeat for a while. The choice must be made to win. The choice must be conscious. It must be made now.
■■■■■■■■■■■■■■■■■■■■■■■■■■■■■■■■■■■■■■

# May 26

*<u>G</u>et familiar with yourself. Don't be afraid to touch yourself and arouse your potential.  –ali-*

Ignorance can only be countered by education, but education is not something you learn by rote or by imitation... Neither is it the syndicated experiences of prime time heroes. Technically, it is your own ability to mandate what is right for you. This, to a nicety, is primitive (natural) education and from it stems the nucleus of your intellectual domain which allows you choices. Suppose you are athletically inclined and your primitive education suggests you have the raw talent to be a football player, then your formalized instruction should happen within that medium instead of having your talent misappropriated at a basketball camp. The same would hold true if you were an accountant. Don't trivialize your energy by being compelled to understand or study info that doesn't relate directly to your sphere of expertise. That is an invasion.  You do not dispel ignorance by simply teaching "something" in an attempt to streamline its aggression. All you're doing is creating a bleak tableau for it to incubate. What has to be done is to refocus priorities so that you can consolidate your primitive education with structured in-line education. Your choices flow from this marriage due mainly to the fact that your direct familiarity with the fundamental issues will provide initiative rather than a decision between the lesser of 2 evils. The bottom line is this: don't get wasted by info you do not need. That's ignorant.

## May 27
### *Choose*

There are no magic choices but here's a tip or 2.

A choice is private development wanting to go public

A choice is the accomplished handiwork of your existing resources offering to do more.

A choice is the proceeds from your efforts taking a trip up.

A choice is an improvement perched atop your decisions.

A choice is an expense account for your career.

■■■■■■■■■■■■■■■■■■■■■■■■■■■■■■■■■■■■■■■■■■

## May 28

### *Lose*

An excursion between the lesser of 2 evils is the unwanted baggage of ignorance, a non-profit organization that feeds off your inability to use your talent to your advantage. It is an under-the-table transaction between you and the environment which controls you. It is a sealed bid that forces you between a rock and a hard place.

## May 29

*The week's lesson in a SNAPSHOT*
*acquire skill.......   >>>>>>>>>Primitive (natural) aptitude
*perfect skill........>>>>>>>>>>direct structured education
*move forward with skill>>>>>learning pertinent information (only)
*grow with skill.... >>>>>>>>>transition of return.
■■■■■■■■■■■■■■■■■■■■■■■■■■■■■■■■■■■

# May 30

*Prisons are Amerikkka's bars and gripes.* —
*ali-*

It has been said that you can measure the morality of a country by the length of the women's hemline. I assert that a country's humanity is reflected in the industry where its minority labors. This directly points to that nation's sensitivity. Look at this country and see how its minority has been dealt with. The three major industries where African-Americans men dominate are the NFL, the NBA, and the B.O.P.(Bureau Of Prisons). We are virtually locked out of any of the great bastions of power since they are not minority-inclusive, and there have been no calls to transform the system. This is in line with the assumption of the Bell Curve which insists that blacks have "brain damage". Where is the humanity in this? African-Americans are penalized in this country for not being role models when, in fact, we represent the model portrayed to us. In the same way that children imitate and internalize the habits of their parents, young black males are the express manifestation of the internalized American spirit. The turf war over commodities (drugs), the guns, the violence. Where did we learn this? Uncle Sam! He has been the ultimate homeboy, gang-banging on an international scale for always, struggling over turf for access to salable commodities (oil). In the hood, we just get down on a local, street level like Uncle Sam does globally. Presumably, he doesn't want to be reminded, but that's why the prisons are full. We just want to be a big, bad bully like our favorite uncle.

■■■■■■■■■■■■■■■■■■■■■■■■■■■■■■■■■■■■■■■■■■■

## May 31

*Ignorance will not ignore you if you don't
practice what you preach.* —ali—

Failure is the perfect choice for people who want to practice being ignorant or who support the notion that good luck is waiting 'round the corner. Sadly, there is no "sweet spot" where everything will turn out just right when there are no plans to capture the opportunities that are paying out the best returns for your efforts.

# June 1

*When you finally get it right, you'll always find*
*that all it takes is what it took.   —ali-*

On the road to self-improvement and success, your attitude is your report card, and from time to time you must march the concepts of your new attitude out in a military-like promenade for inspection. You must carefully assess them, paying particular attention to any that you may have overworked. The problem with this forced labor is that if you tend to overwork a concept, no mater how good it serves you, sooner or later you will take its function for granted and it will become routine. A regimen of monotony will set in and you'll compel this concept to work at no cost, paying it no mind. Usually when this accident occurs, the seeds of failure are given time to germinate because you suddenly neglect your habit of putting your attitude through its paces. Distraction in the midst of anything beckons disaster. Remember that you're never in charge with your attitude on cruise control.

# June 2

*Success is the shortcut that leads to greater success.  —ali-*

Don't drive drunk!  That's what it's like trying to power your way through life with your attitude idling and not working at its peak performance level.  That is a basic missing component that you're never told about in your search for self-discovery; that even after you develop the right stuff attitude-wise, you still must keep it in perfect or at least good working order.  At the free throw line, a basketball player, no matter how many prior shots he has made, never forgets to concentrate. If he desires continued success, he realizes that even with something as routine as a free throw, he cannot become distracted. No matter how many times the approaches the free throw line, he never allows his attitude towards what he is doing to change because he is intent on continued success. Continued maintenance of a winning attitude is sometimes the unwelcome expense of success. Sure, everyone touts the adage about how success will improve your conditions, but what is not even hinted at is the fact that success, in and of itself, is not static. It is a continuum and due to its dynamism, continued success must be pursued in much the same manner as success. We are led to believe that success is the opportunity that leads directly to easy street. Well, not actually.  Success is the shortcut that should lead to continued success.  Betcha no one ever told you that? Success is simply a diploma. You graduate into continued success only when your attitude becomes valedictorian for your life.
■■■■■■■■■■■■■■■■■■■■■■■■■■■■■■■■■■■■■■■■■■■

June 3

*White folks are smart. They know that the best thing about having a job is keeping it.*

*ali-*

It is the American way to laud and applaud the cosmetic veneer of everything and not report on the "accoutrements" or accessories required to make things go. That's just how it goes. Failure is a billion dollar industry so it's left up to you as a duty to look beneath the surface. Failure, too, needs its adherents. Failure works. Failure is the smart bomb of economics. Since everyone can't be successful, it has now become possible for the not nearly successful to profit at the expense of the total failures. And the beat goes on.........

## June 4

*Success is sorta like the morning after. You have to do it again.     –ali-*

So there you have it. The year is ½ past and you're just now learning that in order to be truly successful, you must prepare for the success that comes after success. Betcha your daddy didn't tell you that?  Success ain't nuthin' if you can't keep it coming.  That's why the brotha who robs a bank and gets away with the money scot-free manages to get himself caught days later. He had no idea of how to capitalize on his initial success. He made no plans to be successful after success. All his ingenuity allowed him was the successful acquisition of the money, not the successful use of it. He failed to delve into the hidden intricacy of how to remain successful once the initial success was achieved. He assumed quite wrongly that the total embodiment of success rested upon the accomplished job, not realizing that he must work much harder to sustain his success. Lacking sufficient plans for the aftermath of success is failure.  Ain't that a bitch!

▪▪▪▪▪▪▪▪▪▪▪▪▪▪▪▪▪▪▪▪▪▪▪▪▪▪▪▪▪▪▪▪▪▪▪▪▪▪▪▪▪

## June 5

*Success is a naked mannequin lying inside your soul
waiting on you to dress it up and take it out.      –
ali-*

The real anchor for success is the acknowledgement that before you can conquer cyberspace, you must 1$^{st}$ master innerspace, the seat of your true empire. This simplicity will allow you to develop a refuge against the stress and storm of the toil and strife inherent in the courtship of success. In order to thrive externally, you have to be alive internally. This internal compass is like your personal theme park where all your self-induced strengths play about carefree, waiting to be organized and marketed to your advantage. However much we may protest it, hard work is the go-between that bridges the conceiving with the achieving. That's why reliance on your inner strength is so relevant. A little taste of defeat won't or can't change or disrupt your entire belief system. Once your inner spirit becomes user-friendly, it will become and remain a most astute ambassador to the warp-speed turmoil of the outer world where the actualization of your goals takes shape. Go inside, my people, go inside.

# June 6

*Black folks in America are connoisseurs in the fine art of making other people rich.   —ali-*

A funny thing happened to the African-American on his way to success.   FACTS.   Facts have a strange way of adjusting themselves so that you can't deny them even when they are over 300 years old. And that's a fact. Another more ethnic one is that from the very 1st instance in this country that we were awarded wages or any other type of income, it was associated with consumerism.   The revenue-generating capacity of black dollars were forever geared toward consumption and not structured for the building of industry. From the earliest times, we were forced into a strained wage-earning system with only enough diversity to allow for perhaps a few dollars advance against the next paycheck. Effectively barred from credit, we were shut out from any broad-base economic ventures with the result of our being almost exclusively licensed as consumers and this is our paramount attitude towards the marketplace now.  We relate as buyers of goods. The momentum of this outlook has not changed much since we were pressed into the service of spending instead of investing, of buying instead of selling. Even today, with 750 billion dollars (more than all but 13 countries) we still warm to our role as "yum-yum-eat-'em-ups".  Even though we are the late-comers to the banquet, there is still no need to flirt with hunger. The goodies are there. Instead of checking on competitors who struggle for access to our goldmine, let's make products for ourselves. We know what we like and it will stop the world from laughing at our dependency. Do 4 Self. The future is now.

June 7$^{th}$

*Don't bug yourself. Hug yourself! -Ali-*

It has been proven that some people are self-destructive. They like to experiment, and a wee bit of experimentation is not bad, but when you trespass beyond the prescribed limit into the bold tampering with your own nature, then you will be severely punished. You can't fool Mother Nature, so don't leave home without knowing who you are.

## June 8

*Don't leave home without knowing who you are.*
*—ali—*

In your personal life, if you must constantly refigure odds and rearrange averages after being halfway through the year, then it just may be that you are not a good candidate for success in any of the things you wished to accomplish. Chances are great that you may have subscribed to a set of circumstances that are irrelevant to your true nature. One thing that should be done every December $31^{st}$ is to enter into a congratulatory deal with yourself not to promise anything to yourself that is out of line with your true nature. Now, this presupposes that prior to the $31^{st}$, you have deduced just what your true nature is. If by chance you are a poet trapped inside the guise of a garbage collector, then you should have no reason to expect to be invited to work out with the Carolina Panthers. Such an expectation would be irrelevant, a travesty to your nature, not to mention downright foolish since in such a demand, there is too little capacity for personal success. You are a poet not a football player. When you lock into your latent talent, whatever it is, your nature will greet you enthusiastically, giving you good hard shove towards what you should be doing for the rest of your life. Don't fret. You may not know the substance of your true nature, but it knows you. When you hit home, it will swallow you up in a hug.

## June 9

*For some people, success is learning how to kick dirt in other people's faces.        –ali-*

As part of the deal to seal a long-term pact with your inner spirit, you must also be completely wired for communication with the outside world so that your frame of reference stays current. The point being made is that one should not get lost or confused...      There is a difference between "spiritual" and "religious'. The emphasis is on spiritual because sometimes getting religious narrows your focus and encloses you behind a walled fortress where technology and science are viewed as contrary to God's intent. As such they are hailed as playthings of the devil, and their use is shunned or avoided as much as possible.  In many cases, such a limited viewpoint encapsulates one in a less than realistic snapshot of how change is influenced by advances wrought by the hands of man. This almost forces one to live in a strictly guarded religious cave. Technology exists not as an intrusive public arm of Big Brother, but rather as the price of doing biz'ness in the here and now. Now run and tell that!

## June 10

*Seduction is the strong arm of wanting-to-do-it-anyway.  —ali-*

Don't be seduced into complacency.  Life is a struggle.  So is success. If you don't grasp this, then you had better redefine what you have learned to include this lil' tidbit.  Very rarely will you not be given the grant of a new day that is not impregnated with crisis, whether professional or personal.  And believe it or not, most of it is not unhealthy. Some trials simply coerce you into trusting in your own ability to solve problems.  Other trials daze you, making you stumble as they seek to push you towards oblivion.  It is crisis of this sort that carries the stamp of life and death, and for these you will need a strong inner system of calm. Lacking such, you will jump out of a window.  Believe this, there is nothing magical about losing. Losing entails a definite sense of deprivation and there is no consolation prize to compensate for loss---except one: *The belief that you can bounce back!* And this comes from within. That is why it is very important to cultivate the inner you and to fortify your spiritual resolve. This will be your bunker when the storms come and come they must. Why? Because success demands struggle

## June 11th

*In the real world, u be either thriving, striving, or jiving.*

When it comes to success, there are three kinds of people: they are (1) those who thrive; (2) those who strive; and (3) those who jive. Wanna know how to spot who's who? (1) The highly successful, self-evolved individuals are those who are keyed into the outer world, but also possess a strong inner world. They be thrivin'. (2) These individuals are keyed into the outer world, but lack a secure inner base from which to launch a campaign for personal growth and development. They simply follow the trend of existing from paycheck to paycheck. They be strivin' (3) these characters are not keyed in realistically to the outer world and they also lack an internal foundation. They mostly go to prison. These, they be jivin'.

Choose your #. Are U an Ace? Deuce? Trey?

## June 12

*Think again*

If you think the catalyst for your success is going to be the residual crumbs of someone else's largesse----you're dead wrong. And to minimize confusion, here's why. Men are a monopoly that money dominates.

## June 13

*Beware of the man who provides you with poison,*
*but keeps the antidote to himself.      –ali–*

Put this lil gem among your trinkets: Always keep one eye on the man who hands you poison, but doesn't give you the antidote. And now for the confession of the day. I confess that the "just get it done" ethic is potent poison and its antidote is that it should never be employed when there are more diplomatic options available. This is the safeguard against the abuse or misuse of this poison. It is a power that should never be used when the aims are fruitless or inconsequential. This power belongs to the rule of kings, not extremists. I, once, had an associate who was a firm believer in "Just do it". In any situation, it was the operation of choice until one day when the cops came to arrest him for some petty crime, he chose to shoot it out. Needless to say, he got himself killed. A more suitable option would have been to surrender, go to jail, and make bail. That single option would have led to other options such as hiring a good lawyer or either fleeing to another state. Anyway, the moral of this snapshot is to never accept the poison without accepting the antidote.

# June 14

*You drink water from an idea. You sip champagne from an ideal. –ali–*

The ideal is this. Wherever you are and whatever you are doing in any stage of your development must be decided by the value and effectiveness of what is happening NOW. The force of any plans you make for yourself should be determined by the conditions of NOW and not any past date. This is true whether one intends to sell Chinese food or cocaine. Previous success achieved by someone else may not be applicable in your case since the causes and reasons for the success may no longer prevail. There may no longer be a harvest for Chinese food or cocaine due to a change in taste or the police respectively, so before you aim at seizing power in any sphere of interest, explain your actions by proof that justifies your involvement. A good rule of thumb for the conqueror is that the rewards must outweigh the risks. All efforts must be balanced against your ability to positively control and influence the ultimate end of those efforts. You retain and maintain this control by strategic planning which enables you to manipulate current conditions as they exist NOW. To seize power you are obligated to conduct yourself in a manner derived from your confidence that you deserve power. To be supremely successful, you must specialize in what is right for you. Imported solutions must be discarded. It's you against the world. If you see what you want---- TAKE IT! This is the principle for only the bold. After God----Me.
■■■■■■■■■■■■■■■■■■■■■■■■■■■■■■■■■■■■■■■■■

## June 15

*Inside the 2 minute drill when the game is on the line, everyone is a franchise player.   –ali-*

This is the drill. It's you against the world. No more sparring. What you want may only have wide appeal to you so don't squander time defending your vision to others. You are a Brotherhood of 1 whose primary code of behavior is that you are man enough to stop the world and then take what you want from it! This, in a nutshell, is the code of the Superman Warrior. It is not for those who welcome and accept the conventional tradition of the pie-in-the-sky. Nor is it for any who simply invite renewed failure by sitting under the rich man's table lapping up crumbs like a lazy dog. No, this code is the Way of the Warrior who upholds his right to success by any means necessary. In matters of survival, whether economic or romantic, it makes no difference if the boot on your neck is Timberland or Jimmy Choo.   This does not transfer chic to oppression. No sir, damn the boot. Break the leg of the boot wearer. You cannot pledge yourself to submission simply because the oppressor beats you with a velvet whip. That promotes your weakness because usually when you're getting whipped it means you are not fighting back. The Superman Warrior looks to the future with confidence and he never takes the long way home

## June 16

*A greater menace is not what the poor will do for money, but what the rich will do with it. —ali-*

Whether you like it or not, you are at war. All of us are soldiers in the war against poverty and there is only one natural resource against being poor and that is MONEY!

■ ■ ■ ■ ■ ■ ■ ■ ■ ■ ■ ■ ■ ■ ■ ■ ■ ■ ■ ■ ■ ■ ■ ■ ■ ■ ■ ■ ■ ■ ■ ■ ■ ■ ■ ■ ■ ■ ■ ■ ■ ■ ■

## June 17

*Givin' the black man 40 acres and a mule would have been tantamount to givin' him the world.  –*
*ali-*

Once launched, the scramble for money has superseded everything else in this country. Remember this fact. It is money that has encouraged the white man to exploit us and our lack of money that discourages us from doing anything about it.
■■■■■■■■■■■■■■■■■■■■■■■■■■■■■■■■■■■■■■■■■■■

## June 18

*All sport ain't play.    –ali–*

Check this Snapshot out. It has been said (by me) that if you really want to see where a man is coming from, investigate his actions when he is at play. In the same way that a player brings his jock-strap to the arena, he also brings his personality. His mode of play usually mirrors his persona. The selfish ball hog on the basketball court is likewise greedy and selfish off the court. The team player is loyal both on and off the court. The good defensive player is as tenacious in guarding his ideas and goals as he is with guarding his on-court opponents. Your personality, once formed, is your individual drum major. No matter what you're e doing, it is never absent. Sports have become so big in the country that it has become an alter ego, a polished mirror for what actually is going on, but you have to recognize the parallels. Welcome to the sportin' life.

## June 19

*Misinformation is like rigor mortis. That's why the black man's head is so hard. –ali–*

Were you set up inadvertently to fail by what your parents taught or didn't teach you? You play the game according to how you were coached to play, but what if your coach didn't fully grasp the mechanics of the game or how to evolve a winning strategy within the framework of the established rules. When a winning strategy isn't evolved, it is not the ones actually playing the game that are suspect. It is the coaches. For whatever reason, the players couldn't function competitively because they were given ineffective instructions and misinformation which caused them to fail. The players had the skillz: they merely lacked proper guidance. On a personal level, when your parents send you into the game of life with improper coaching, you will fail no matter how skilled you are. So examine what your coaches (Mom & Dad) told you and dismiss it if it is misinformation. Don't blame your parents. They were taught by their parents who were taught by their parents whose parents were probably slaves taught by the slavemasters. Only when you know the truth can you play the game as it was meant to be played.

## June 20

*Don't be fooled by your own foolishness*　　　-
　　　　　　　　　　　　　　　　　　*ali-*

Lacking intimate contact with yourself always increases the possibility that you will end up keeping up with the many ways of selling yourself short. That much is certain. Why? Because you cannot budget ignorance! When you attempt to adapt to the changing landscape of ignorance without a sense of knowing that you are simply a well-heeled patron of your own inner darkness, you are merely accumulating credit as your own personal special-kind-of-fool

## June 21

*The only time it is wise to go for yourself is when you can do for yourself.   –ali-*

Although all men conduct themselves in basically the same way, the Superman Warrior allows himself a certain critical distinction.  He never places anyone's interests above his own.  To do so would indenture him to someone else and the Superman Warrior could never exist in such a climate.  The fact that he resists forced labor in the service of another does not in any fashion indicate selfishness because contained in and intertwined with his interests and needs are also the interests and needs of his woman and family.  There is no separation between his interests and theirs. When his wife needs, he needs, when his children need shoes, it is he who needs and all of their interests are manned by his burning desire to meet any need at the point of contact----and destroy it!  Largely, by this method does the Superman Warrior provide stability at home because when he concentrates on his interests alone, all other necessary needs are likewise met, and recognized. For the Superman Warrior, it is not ever a conquest for bread and butter, frocks and shoes. Instead, for him, the struggle is for the world to give him what he wants. This is the way of the Superman Warrior...

*June 22*

*In life, the 1-2-3s are just as important as the A-B-C's so while you're learning to string together the alphabets, don't forget to learn your "numbers" because you may have to count on your mouth to save your ass. —ali—*

More about the Superman Warrior later, perhaps. In lesser men, your habits of work are derived from the duties imposed upon you by others and oftentimes it is these cumbersome duties that lure you into an economic situation you cannot endure. You can never beat the market without the capacity to understand your own potential. Potential is not good luck or a wing and a prayer. It is the talent to capture all your resources and then tie them up in a joint venture with your abilities to unveil success. You will be deemed responsible for accomplishing this bit of premeditated wisdom and it will help determine how far away you are from being a Superman Warrior. Ace....Deuce....Trey

## June 23

*When the whistle blows, it is time to go home.  —ali-*

Expand your horizons. To truly have a vested interest in personal growth, you may sometimes have to redraw the borders of your frontier and learn to function in new ways. After sorting through their many behavioral options, many individuals find they have chosen a mode of existence that was not totally conducive or complementary with what they should be doing. Usually, they become aware of this late in life. Others more fortunate realize it earlier and immediately drop out of the rat race  to follow their heart. That's why many corporate executives are tuning out and becoming artists or mountain climbers. They wanted to do what suits them. When you are stuck in the wrong profession, your conscience will act as a whistle-blower, giving you a reality check. To ignore the whistle in light of your unhappiness with what your present behavior allots you is like compelling your soul to suffer indigestion. Get out. Go Home. Don't let your occupation seize your life and squeeze out all the happiness.

## June 24

*Ain't no way to protect your head when your heart
ain't in it. —ali-*

. WHEN WORK MAKES A MAN
MISERABLE, MISERY FOLLOWS HIM HOME.
■■■■■■■■■■■■■■■■■■■■■■■■■■■■■■■■■■■■■■■

# June 25

*Don't cash your check until your wife is happy.  —
ali-*

You cannot cheat the hangman.  In the long run, unhappiness on the job is an ad for a custody battle over who gets the kids after the divorce.  Do not consider a promotion a tactical victory when it has been won at the expense of your family stability.  A    promotion under those circumstances is little more than corporate welfare, and a job that steals from your ability to create happiness at home is a robber baron.  You balk and bark at in-laws whenever they attempt to influence what goes on your home, but you offer no protest at your boss' ability to shape your domestic policy by controlling your attitude. 80% of most stress is job-related and over time, it affects the real issues at home, obscuring them or disguising them until they either explode or implode.  Since you're not aware of the true origin of the stress, you are powerless to counter it. You are the hapless victim of an on-the-job agenda that detonated in your home. You vehemently oppose landmines on foreign soil, but yet you permit your bossman to plant them throughout your home. Don't be deceived.  The job has not lost its power to preside over the affairs of your after-hour activities. Check this out.  If you can survive in an environment where your talent is not appreciated, you can thrive in one where your talent is welcomed.

# June 26

*If it ain't a necktie, don't go 'round wearing a noose around your neck. —ali—*

To escape the hangman's noose, you must, of a necessity, employ the technique of *dynamic structuring* to your re-program of economic development. This technique involves the setting up of a timetable that regulates and limits the use of your talent or skill in a particular market for a specific period of time. If, at the end of that period, you have not maximized your goals or acquired a certain level of job satisfaction, then you move on to the next level in your program. In order to render accurate assumptions, you need only to isolate a pair of factors on your flow chart. . (1) GOAL REALIZATION and (2) JOB SATISFACTION. By carefully monitoring data from both factors, at period's end, you should have no problem with their configuration on the chart. If the liaisons between the two factors fail to verify your legitimacy in that particular industry, you go on to the next rung of your structure. By pursuing other projects, you can best capitalize on all areas of your expertise. Even your hobbies may prove lucrative. *Dynamic structuring* is a provocative device against the mental exploitation of the corporate world and a defense against the collapse of family life. The inherent ability to stimulate your talent in the job market according to plan keeps you stimulated and challenged because you know there is something beyond the present. This creates a much needed gap in your job's control over you and your capacity to function off the job. Carefully prepared, *dynamic structuring* can help you beat the blasé and the blues of the 9-5 work world.

## June 27

### *Meet Trey*

Remember the drill from June 11th?  Well, meet Trey. Check him out.  He's the type of brotha with his face always screwed up in a permanent frown as if he's forever ready to yell "ouch!" This is because he is the eternal victim of his own foolishness. He is always knee-deep in his own word-of-mouth- testimony about how good it is going to be when his ship comes in. During the interim, however, his ideas of wealth rest upon the amount of money he is able to sponge from family and friends. He has keen infrared sensors that allow him to ferret out a free lunch, but outside of his personalized realm of begging, he is clueless about the social dynamics of life. He is not adapted to the inner world of his affections and emotions where the common sense strategies for survival exist, and lacking refinement, his crude contact with the external realm marks him as an outsider.  On the big screen of life, Trey is recognized as background noise. Treys are usually divided into different camps.  Those that go to jail and those who simply bump into things because their eyes are closed. Whenever he wakes up or gets out of jail, feed him, give him a dollar or two, and then send him on his way. He be jivin'

■■■■■■■■■■■■■■■■■■■■■■■■■■■■■■■■■■■■■■■■■■■■■■■

## June 28

### *Meet Deuce*

Deuce is the brotha with the lop-sided architecture. He is visually aware and verbally cued into what is transpiring in the external world, but he lacks the inner strength of a moral foundation, so he is like a pretty red Cadillac with a lawnmower engine. He is constantly baffled by the fact that his wheels spin, but when he needs to get ahead, there is no traction. His success is hinged upon the fact that he is expert in following orders and can professionally mimic truly successful individuals. He just can't get around much due to his problem with mobility (vision). The chief objective of his strategy for anything is the proverbial huffing and puffing or throwing his weight around. Deuce is increasingly and aggressively competitive as long as the work is at arm's length and nothing truly cerebral is required. Deuce has brawn so he'll always be in demand at construction sites and tough man contests. He be strivin'

■■■■■■■■■■■■■■■■■■■■■■■■■■■■■■■■■■■■■■■■■■■■■■■■

## *June 29*

### *Meet Ace*

Ace fully enjoys success and all its far-flung implications. He doesn't appreciate the need for wild cards or lucky hunches, but yet he expects increasing returns and accelerated growth from all his ventures, whether professional or personal. He nurtures his woman with the same intensity that he reserves for his stock portfolio. He is so well-evolved that he is not shut out from any of life's experiences. He is solidly at the center of his inner and outer universe where he is a spontaneous participant in the joys of both. Due to his reliance on his internal compass to guide him through the atmosphere of external choice, he is fundamentally sound. He lags behind nothing or no one, and is sufficient unto himself without the need for intermediaries to remind him of his worth. Forever, as such, he is thrivin'.

June 30

## <u>NO ONE NEED SPEAK FOR THE SUPERMAN WARRIOR!!!</u>

## *July 1*

Conjecture and bullshit aside, we need to devise our own political philosophy. We need to develop a nationalistic approach to our dilemma where we are all-inclusive and non-geographical. We are 1! Many of our practical problems could be resolved more efficiently if we were attracted to them with a view to solving them rather than to studying them. What we need is an African-American equivalent of Los Alamos, a real BMW (Black Mentors Working) where our talented $10^{th}$ is not afraid to think outside the box. BMWs mission must be not only to ponder possibilities, but to devise and develop programs to eliminate our technological and political awkwardness. BMW must work to heal the split personality of the black collective and our recovery must be viewed in fresh, imaginative ways. Dig this. Why should we feel obligated to live somewhere where we are powerless? As an option, we should shop around for a city or state, and move in en masse. At BMW, through their study and research of the economic and political structure of certain locales, they could target one so we could move in with enough numbers to control the social machinery with our votes and assume power. After we have secured the city, we repeat the process elsewhere. Just think, we can transform our destiny by "Votes without Borders".

## July 2

Though out large numbers had its roots in a partnership that had nothing to do with the technical strategy of a voting bloc, we must discuss how best to exercise this clout. It is a boon we have created for ourselves and though we may not have had the vaguest idea of what we were doing, we had better take advantage of this opportunity. We sponsored it and we should benefit from it. Now is the time to embrace new methods of empowerment. We have followed the divine prescription to "go forth and multiply" eagerly. Now, let's turn the power of the womb into real political power.

## July 3

In truth, the strength and effectiveness of any infamous occurrence can be measured by what happens in the interval before the genuine progress of the experience and the victims' preparedness to thwart it.    Oftentimes, the victims don't-see-it-coming or have no idea what-in-the-hell-hit-them because they were not paying attention.    Sound familiar?  It should be. Black people have not been vigilant and if we don't stop sleeping at the wheel, our wake up call will continue to be the pathetic refrain of…."Damn, why me"
■■■■■■■■■■■■■■■■■■■■■■■■■■■■■■■■■■■■■■■■■

## July 4

## Mr. Charlie, Jim Crow, & Uncle Sam

*Once there were 3 brothers*
*Who loved one another?*
*All through thick and thin*
*One day said Charlie, the oldest*
*To Jimmy, the boldest*
*What do you think about sin?*
*Jimmy replied, I don't know about that*
*I'd rather pull rabbits out of a hat*
*Or perform some other sleight-of-hand*
*Sammy shouted me too*
*But what about you*
*After all, you're the head of this Klan*
*Charlie smiled as he spoke*
*Boys, this ain't no joke*
*But a nigga just might be the ticket*
*To help us claw our way to the top*
*If the supply does not stop*
*"Cause black gold is a sure money fix-it*
*Well, boys, ol'Charlie sees it like this*
*A Nigga is a better catch than a fish*
*Better'n than eggs from a young golden hen*
*You don't say, Sammy rasped*
*Thank you, Jesus, Jimmy gasped*
*Plus he's stronger than any ten men*
*We're in the money, Charlie cried*
*But both his brothers had already surmised*
*What this new deal was all about*
*Charlie would put niggas in chains*
*And Jimmy would drive 'em insane*
*While Sammy helped turn 'em out*
*It was a plan they agreed*
*A damn fine one indeed*
*And the niggas would have hell to pay*
*As Charlie worked them in the fields*
*While Jimmy passed all the bills*
*But Sammy still has them today*

■■■■■■■■■■■■■■■■■■■■■■■■■■■■■■■■■■■■■■■■■■■

## July 5

As always, existential conditions deem that growth be observed before any change be acknowledged or allowed, and this holds true throughout the entire spectrum of life, encompassing the plant and animal kingdom as well. No matter how much it shows off, a rosebud is not a rose until there is the required growth. Or no matter how much it can eat or how fast it can run, a pony's status is undisturbed until it actually evolves into a horse. In either case, the transformation is legitimate only when the correct amount of growth is observed. It is this "natural" formula that has eluded us as a people. We still think and believe we are who they say we are and living down to someone else's criteria is a dirty deed done dirt cheap that we commit on ourselves. We're such smooth criminals, Ha!

## July 6

Somewhere along the way, we gave birth to the notion that we could deserve a new attitude without the possibilities of new values. It doesn't work like that. Besides the new millennium will mark a veritable shift in the conditions under which both our attitudes and values will grow up... And what you are going to discover just like white folks did is that there ain't no easy way to be free. Freedom has a price, and you can't put it on lay-a-way. You either take it or you remain a slave.
■■■■■■■■■■■■■■■■■■■■■■■■■■■■■■■■■■■■■■■■■■

## July 7

You must ask yourself, how you get caught up in the hoopla of the celebration a few days ago when your situation is strictly identical to what it was 300 years ago? We are still chained and bound. We are still officially sanctioned for being black. We are not free.

■■■■■■■■■■■■■■■■■■■■■■■■■■■■■■■■■■■■■■■■■■■■

## July 8

Ain't no easy way to be free! As so often happens, the struggle to right wrongs will test everything a people have, but when that people clings dearly to the idea that their freedom is worth fighting for, it's all good. They will come to know that, simply put, they will have to use what they've got to get what they want. This brings up this vital observation. Hold on to your hat because you ain't heard this before. Here goes. Black book clubs could be the 1$^{st}$ step in improving our chances for future success because as historic as they are, they can also be heroic. How? By evolving into Black Think Tanks! Why? Because the time has come to utilize the immense brain trust of black women. And that may turn out to be our greatest secret weapon yet.
▪▪▪▪▪▪▪▪▪▪▪▪▪▪▪▪▪▪▪▪▪▪▪▪▪▪▪▪▪▪▪▪▪▪▪▪▪▪▪▪▪▪▪▪

# July 9

And now for those of us who may think that Think Tanks are not worth thinking about, why don't you think about this. Think Tanks are a completely reliable way of assessing problems and defining solutions. And in case you're deaf, dumb, and blind it was Think Tanks that landed us in the hot water we're in today. The first white Think Tank, Rand, was established to find creative solutions to the problems associated with WWII. This group, in Santa Monica, California, ushered in the age of nuclear weapons. In short order, after the war, other Think Tanks sprung up, one at MIT among them. Only now they fixed their sights on a social problem: What to do with the Negro. In 1975, I was privileged to view a Think Tank study paper. The report concluded, in sum, that the black male must be set up to fail. Needless to say, putting brothas in prison was designed as a mode of operation for white Amerikkka as part of the solution to fix the black man. In 1988, I sought out a second Think Tank paper. By now, the quest to fix the black man was more urgent. In this no-holds barred paper, it was mapped out that by the year 2000; they wanted prisons to be filled with black men. They also advanced the idea of creating a rift between brothas and sistas. How, you ask, was this rift to be engineered? Simple. They would swing open the doors of the corporate world to sistas which would invariably guarantee economic disparity which they presumed would destroy compatibility among sistas and brothas. It has. The Black American Princesses (BAPs) of the corporate world don't want no broke nigga. Thanks to white Think Tanks, we are living a nightmare. To counter, we need our own Think Tanks. Now!

## July 10

Think on this. What is true enough is that we must acknowledge the desperation of our plight? This should not be difficult given the pitiless iron fist of those who oppose us. Worse yet is the contradiction of the Hispanic question. Will they prove to be another foe politically? Will all African-Americans be swept out of office as we get out-voted by Hispanics who now out-number us in this country? What happens to the powerless when they become even more powerless? Can't be nuthin' nice.

■■■■■■■■■■■■■■■■■■■■■■■■■■■■■■■■■■■■■■■■■■■■■■■

## July 11

Don't sit on the sideliners. The greatest tragedy and only real risk in life is to sit on the sidelines, a spectator in the affairs of the world. There is no worst scenario than this because life is geared for your active participation, so sitting on the sidelines should make you feel uncomfortable. Don't do failure. Get into the game of life. Play 2 win.

## July 12

No one is born with a built-in life strategy based on absolute failure. You're an architect and you're equipped with exactly the right tools to perform the duties assigned you by the Creator, and among your assets is the ability to think as well as the right to ask questions.. Only problem is, we sometimes fail to think and minus correct thinking, the right questions can never be verbalized. Due to this fault, you forfeit your chances of success and settle for, at best, the incredibly foolish hope that a closed mouth will get fed. It ain't happening.
∎ ∎ ∎ ∎ ∎ ∎ ∎ ∎ ∎ ∎ ∎ ∎ ∎ ∎ ∎ ∎ ∎ ∎ ∎ ∎ ∎ ∎ ∎ ∎ ∎ ∎ ∎ ∎ ∎ ∎ ∎ ∎ ∎ ∎ ∎ ∎ ∎

## *July 13*

Starting this moment, you must understand that you are a brand name and not some cheap, knock-off imposter of your best friend, idol, or your mentor. You must give full expression to your creativity and your brainpower, remembering that there is no pressure to succeed when you don't want shit. Call it what you will, but there will forever be ample opportunities to be a failure, so don't ever allow yourself to become anonymous in your own affairs. Take the initiative to salute yourself. You're a soldier. And there's a war going on.

## July 14

The idea of black folks taking care of our biz'ness is an idea that needs promoting, so like it or not, we have got to be all about it. Whatever it takes to inspire us to take action is what must be done. Let's make no mistake about that. Doing anything is better than doing nothing because a good try can turn into the spiritual and/or political road map that will get us moving in the right direction. When you're fighting back and doing for yourself, the ugliness of life will suddenly reveal that it has a second skin because unlike beauty, freedom is not skin deep. Freedom, my brothas and sistas, is the lifeblood of living well. And living well is the best revenge.

■■■■■■■■■■■■■■■■■■■■■■■■■■■■■■■■■■■■■■■■■■

## July 15

Without big ambitions, our historical record will continue to be one of abject failure. Again, it bears repeating in case you missed my drift that we need 2 things. (1) An ideology that defines us and (2) an agenda that defines our ideology. Both entail re-positioning ourselves squarely in the middle of the fight for a piece of the American pie-----not just with other minorities, but with the elitist white clique that calls the shots in this country. We must raise our expectations, streamline our internal differences, and rejuvenate our collective spirit. Starting now, our policies must be developed unilaterally. We can still forge alliances whenever they serve our interests. But our major task is to become strong enough so, if need be, we can compete with any other people for whatever resources we must have to extend our power.

## July 16

And there it is.  Power.  That's what it's all about. Power.  Black people had better grasp this. No matter how much we detest governmental confrontation, we must make choices.  The post September 11 future will present us fewer chances to make choices and the danger in this is that the more Uncle Sam turns into a control freak, the more he will be fortified by our complacency.  If we don't step it up, then we'll continue to be shoeshine boys in the global marketplace.  Incidentally, being a shoe-shine boy ain't no come up even if you were previously a bootlicker. The trick, black folks, is not simply to get the boot off your neck but to put the shoe on the other foot-----our feet!

■■■■■■■■■■■■■■■■■■■■■■■■■■■■■■■■■■■■■■■■

## *July 17*

Papa got a brand new bag. Seriously. Across black America, abandonment is an awful evil and it must be contested. Brothas must assume full responsibility for their families and running away must cease. We are no longer n the plantation, but the mental chains have not yet been broken. It must be remembered that the black man was divested of his right to be a daddy by the courts and every white man in the south invested considerable time and energy into making sure the law was fulfilled. Niggas could not be fathers!

The fact remains that we must and should be incensed and disgusted by the failure of black men to stand up and support their families, but we should also be incensed and disgusted at the apparatus that set the trend into motion. The healing must start at the wound.
∎∎∎∎∎∎∎∎∎∎∎∎∎∎∎∎∎∎∎∎∎∎∎∎∎∎∎∎∎∎∎∎∎∎∎∎∎∎∎∎∎∎∎

## July 18

As long as there is no attempt to prick the skin of this historic "Daddy be gone" malaise, then anything we do will only have a band-aid effect. It is evident that the sentiment of that centuries old law that declared that there was no such recognizable condition as black fatherhood is still alive and well today. The wound still festers. The law was designed to maim the black man, to reduce him as worthless in his own eyes, to eviscerate him morally, and it was this psychic emasculation that took a big chunk out of black fatherhood. Ain't it a bitch that niggas are home and comfortable in any 'hood except fatherhood! The white man done it up big that time.

## *July 19*

To complicate matters even more is the fact that Black America is not a seamless world. We are a colony within borders where our survival hinges on unraveling the issues that separate us and to get actively involved in all the things that should bind us as a nation. This, by no stretch of the imagination, has to be the near-impossible task it would appear to be if we practice the principle of utility: to utilize the greatest good for the greatest amount of people,

## July 20

The United States Committee for Economic Development after WWII devised a study stating "that in order to keep the cost of labor low, it is necessary to entice or force country people to move into the cities" This, the Committee promised was the method by which there would always be a pool of people who would be nothing but consumers, In addition, the Committee insisted that since they would be both poor and landless, they would also be susceptible to paltry wages. Sounds kinda like us, huh? Man, Mr. Charlie saw us coming and had our number. Now, that's superior game.

■■■■■■■■■■■■■■■■■■■■■■■■■■■■■■■■■■■■■■■■■■■

## July 21

Being powerless murders the soul. One reason is because it allows you no place where you can feel in control. Too bad, it ain't no MySpace for niggas who ain't got no place. Sadly, there is no haven for people whose lives offer them no tangible rewards. When desperation is your primary caretaker, handle it or do something about it. Don't complain----change.

## July 22

Maintaining the commitment to change your life takes time because we do the same thing day in and day out until it becomes part of an almost mechanized routine. And old habits die hard, but it is about opening up to new concepts and new ways of looking at your life. Sometimes it is difficult to stick with our changes, but you can't get caught up in the pattern of resisting change because that is an emotional merry-go-round that will do nothing but keep you going in a circle.

## July 23

*Celebrate.* You should incorporate as much fanfare as possible into your coming-out-of-darkness party. Have a gift-giving ceremony for yourself. *Rejoice.* Decorate your new existence by anointing yourself with a new name. *Sing.* You are the latest newcomer to the community of the aware and it is vital that your arrival be noted and acknowledged, so make it authentic and real. Your very 1st contribution to yourself and others is that everyone knows you are here. *Shout.* Affirm the moment by embedding it into the memorable affairs of the universe. Embellish it with the involvement of all your significant others so that they can honor your rebirth. *Roar.*

## July 24

We must rescue ourselves. This is not jargon or cheap talk. It is an authentic affirmation of what we must do as a people to sustain ourselves because if we do not become more the champion of our own survival, we will surely die. Ain't no bullshit about that. In our bid for self-renewal, one of the 1st things we must is to stop defending the stereotypes against us. We must eradicate the framework of these myths at the same time recognizing the socio/economic structures that helped spawned them. It's time for us to turn off the "stereo" But Stayed tuned.

## July 25

All bullshit aside, there is a deuce of very essential things that we must cozy up to. (1) That our lives are influenced by habit and (2) that habits are shaped by memory. What this means is that our memory (collective) is our enemy. Why? Because we inherited the habit of viewing ourselves as powerless in relation to the white people and we cull from our historical memory, the images to support this sense of helplessness. Habit teaches us how to bring the world into focus; however memory forces us to see the world, not as it really is, but as we are conditioned to see it. So as long as we continue to peek at ourselves through the prism of stereotypes, all we will see is lack and all we will get is psychological abuse. That's just how deep the bullshit goes. We have got to turn off the "stereo". Or else.

■■■■■■■■■■■■■■■■■■■■■■■■■■■■■■■■■■■■■■■■

## July 26

Pity the fool who doesn't understand that the way we see the world controls the way we behave because it is our perceptions that dictate how we interpret our surroundings, so there won't be much we can do to alter our situation until we change our perceptions about what it is we see. But how can you see straight when all you see are stereotypes which have you seeing: cross-eyed? They're vicious and they dissemble a people's self-esteem. They have to be contested. What they can't be is written off. Stereotypes must be challenged. Defeated. Killed. No ifs, ands or buts about it.
■■■■■■■■■■■■■■■■■■■■■■■■■■■■■■■■■■■■■■■■■■■■■■

## July 27

Stereotypes, mind you, are hardly frail. Rather, they are the buffed-up, muscle-bound he-men in a governmental circus act and theoretically, they are worth their weight in gold. Tell me this. How in the hell did the stereotype that niggas are lazy ever take root? How did that happen, especially since we were fresh out of slavery and had practically built the whole damned south? I guarantee that there was no such thing as a lazy slave! This is one stereotype the white man should not have been able to deliver, but he did. Told you, the white man is a master of game.

## July 28

Renewable energy. That's what our children are. Renewable energy. However in order to achieve or to reach their full potential, we must not permit them to get used up and ultimately burnt out because if this infamy occurs they wont emerge as suitable stand-ins for our survival. How can they formulate the visionary concepts needed to reflect our demands for independence when we're not teaching them? All they see is our failure and soon they will be in a position to repeat history. Soon, it will be too late to yell OOPS. That means we had better save the children so they can save us. God bless the child that has his own.

■■■■■■■■■■■■■■■■■■■■■■■■■■■■■■■■■■■■■■■■■■■■■■■

## *July 29*

Predictably, our agenda for the 21$^{st}$ century can't be pieced together with worn out plans borrowed from our old attempts to get something going. Those plans got us nowhere and to date we have been the surrogate fathers of so many mishaps that we appear socially and politically crippled. We have to stop it. Our agenda need not be anything extravagant or exotic, but it has to include the view of ourselves as a globally emerging nation and to bust a move to protect and invest our GNP (Gross National Product). We must, by and large, produce jobs. Anything else would be like playing piano in the dark.

## July 30

As African-Americans, when we start to consider that coming-in-last is a stunningly frightening place to be, then all that will be left for us to do will be to go cold turkey on our obsessive addiction to civil rights. (We need human rights) Life is no beggars' banquet. It is a feast with a full menu.  So we eat, drink, and be merry---or we starve.  The cook is in the kitchen!
■■■■■■■■■■■■■■■■■■■■■■■■■■■■■■■■■■■■■■■■■

# July 31

*How did I go from being a brotha to a dog?*
*Was it much harder than turning a prince into a frog?*
*Or was it that there was no love left for me*
*Or did people enjoy ignoring the person I could be*
*How did I go from being a brotha to a dog?*
*Did the world think I was nothing but a knot upon a log?*
*Couldn't anyone recognize that my cries were just a plea?*
*Not a shout or a whisper, but only my desire to be free*
*How did I go from being a brotha to a dog?*
*And who gave the consent that I could be butchered like a hog*
*What did they expect as I passed my days alone in pain?*
*To whoop, shout or act happy and put locks upon my brain*
*Is a slave forever as slave with his freedom far from sight?*
*Where endless labor fills my days and where nightmares come at night*
*So who says it isn't madness for those who slip behind the fog*
*In a place where they know the secret of turning a brotha into a dog!!!!!!*

## *August 1*

*Death is life with its luck run out.   —ali-*

Another reason why black folk fail so consistently is that our collective consciousness is death-oriented. This is especially true of the young urban males of the race. For them, death is no longer represented as the actual period at the end of life. It is now promoted as the authorizing penalty for any mistake made, however slight. To our youth, death is simply accepted as the ultimate criticism mandated against their actions. As such, it produces a brutal disparity between the length of time they assume they have to live and the actual time they may actually have. This prevailing attitude is patently inconsistent with success. Rather is a guide or a measurement for how much violence they can inflict or withstand. Success for them is fixed within the harsh provision of death missing them. In essence, death is nothing more than life with its luck run out. How does one succeed when they think that death is just around the corner?

■■■■■■■■■■■■■■■■■■■■■■■■■■■■■■■■■■■■■■■■■■■■■■■

## August 2

*Death is a divinely-imposed procedural safeguard against man getting too full of himself.   —ali-*

Death should be the appropriate judge to limit what we accomplish. Not life!  Black people got it ass-backwards. We grant life the power and authority to impose specific, detailed restrictions on what we can and cannot do when the sky should be the limit. We run from life and court death, the exact reverse of the proviso for existence.  Life, when done freely, should offer no restraints, and should impose no constraints other than those issued by God. We impose unnecessary hardships on ourselves by disavowing our right to live effectively.  We can live freely when we learn to live fully. **Live**.  .  U do not have to take overt action to stifle your growth and potential. That the job of death. It is your responsibility to rejoice, to whoop, to holla, to delight in the joy and beauty of being alive**. Live**. Why not? No matter how much you patronize death, it is never more or less susceptible to your actions. It comes when it is time. And only then. **Live.**

August 3

*No matter how much you taunt him, the Grim reaper will not arrive before the proper time*
*-ali*

Wanna be down with a well-kept secret? Well, dig this. *There is no such thing as a premature death!* Death is a divine consideration imposed by God upon each of his creatures. It is not an arbitrary or capricious decree that is subject to anything other than what has been ordained by God Almighty to occur at a precise time. Death, no matter how common or heinous, is not influenced by anything other than God's decree. Man can neither anticipate it nor delay it; never will it be susceptible or even vulnerable to our individual attempt to call it in existence. No one has that power. Only God does. He determines who lives and who dies as well as the time and place of death. Not a single person has died or ever will die before their time. We sadly bemoan the death of a baby as premature, but that isn't so. No death is premature and no one dies early. We die in time with God's decree regardless of how soon after birth it transpires. Don't weaken your hold on life and it auxiliary joys by indulging in a mindset that is inconsistent with divine law. You cannot die before your time and no matter how tough you may think you are, your actions will not tempt God to alter his decree which was firmly fixed before your 1$^{st}$ breath. So, there it is. Hopefully, you'll recognize the pathetic foolishness of living life without a success plan, tinkering with the false notion that you may die before your time. Ha! What you gonna do when you keep on waking morning after morning waiting on death and finally realize you old as hell and ain't got shit. Better get with the program and being stop bamboozled. *Live.*
■ ■ ■ ■ ■ ■ ■ ■ ■ ■ ■ ■ ■ ■ ■ ■ ■ ■ ■ ■ ■ ■ ■ ■ ■ ■ ■ ■ ■ ■ ■ ■ ■ ■ ■ ■ ■ ■ ■ ■ ■ ■ ■

*August 4*

*The 'death around the corner' mentality ain't nuthin' but an updated hip-hop version of the ol' pie in the sky.*
*–ali–*

African-Americans became isolated from any real, meaningful ideas of coping with a successful lifestyle when we were introduced to the old pie-in-the-sky theology offered by countless black preachers. This wait-and-get-ours in the ol' bye and bye made our lives on earth more susceptible to the manipulation and influence of those who put forth this spiritual device to induce our passivity. This church-sponsored doctrine was an assault against our collective will and it confined us to a sort of mental paralysis and belief that our collective existence was a combination of "here-comes-the-white-man" and "waiting on Jesus". It adjusted our sight on death as a reward for our suffering. Take note of this. Death is not a reward. We do not have to earn it by suffering. Death is our inalienable right. In essence, we became the victims of a scheme that tricked us into accepting a price tag on death. We suffered nobly, feeling convinced that the crown Jesus had waiting on us in the hereafter would make our misery and failure worthwhile. Is the picture any clearer now as to where the hip-hop nation inherited their "death-around –the-corner" mentality? They saw their grandparents live it... A standby death where you stand by and wait on Jesus is no worse than a drive by shooting. In both, we enforce our roles as helpless victims. It's time to stop the sadness. Let's end our long time relationship with death as a 'papa", looking to him as a caretaker. He is merely the child of life. Let him go about his biz'ness. Trust me; he knows when to come home.

## August 5

*Though death may possess the power to end our lives, it should never have the power to control it.*
*-ali=*

Let's make things clear. Black people empower death and by so doing, we disallow our use of life to be functional. The results being that we fail to profit from the utility of existence, placing the complete validity of our being into a sponsorship under the negative auspices of death. At all stages of our collective existence, we live as though the glass is half empty (rather than half full) and this unconventional bird's eye view of our mindset raises the specter that we furnish our lives with ineffective living requirements that negate success. We are a death-specific people. As such, we fashion the specifics of our future under the duress of not "making it to the promised land" , and we entitle ourselves to piecemeal subsidies and handouts, claiming them as victories. Instead we must look beyond the record of death and dispute its claim over the manner by which we collectively bargain with life. We must grant death only the power to end our lives, not the power to control it. Then, as a people, we can build for success.

## August 6

*Death is not a passing grade when you have squandered your life, needlessly provoking it to lie down with dogs.* —ali—

Fiddle with this piece of information. Our collective waiting on death is a convenient way of linking us to instant gratification. All our goals are very short term since living conditions in this country have always made note that we may not witness the future. Given this limited world view, we are compelled to plan accordingly as all the peoples of the world are apt to plan in strict accord with their world view. The circumstances and conditions of their lives will evolve via this worldview, so know this. Whenever it plainly shows on the face of a people's actions that they cannot control their environment, they will most definitely be controlled by it! It is a law of nature that men should examine their conditions and then breathe life into the merits of their right to be by imposing their will upon that environment until they triumph. Personally, black people are still operating on a subsidiary plan because somehow it has eluded us that success is not found among the tombstones.

*Remember the dinosaur.*

Study the model below: A people are death-oriented if (1) they fail to educate their children, and (2) they show blatant disrespect for their women. It is not possible for any people to engage in either of the above and survive. How can it even be expected when they (1) kill those among them who have reached the age of serious work, (2) kill the potential of the ones growing up by not teaching them, and (3) destroy the future of the unborn by not reaching out and nurturing the women who are the Mothers of the race? Do you get the picture?
▪▪▪▪▪▪▪▪▪▪▪▪▪▪▪▪▪▪▪▪▪▪▪▪▪▪▪▪▪▪▪▪▪▪▪▪▪▪▪▪▪

## August 8

*One thing about a good myth or lie is that they
know when to be quiet.   –ali-*

We can change the course of this reason for our
failing by altering our thinking process. Think life.
And follow these road rules. (1) be substantially of
one mind where death is concerned, (2) specify
definite reasons for living other than breathing, (3)
justify those specifics by claiming them as
legitimate causes of action, and (4) cautioning
everyone else to get the hell out of our way! When
we are finally able to make a peace treaty with
death, we will have cured one of the fundamental
defects of our invalidated living habits which have
been our most crippling disability. It should be
noted that we as a people cannot subsist on the
merits of such an ideal and it must be dismantled. It
prescribes conditions of defeat. The inadequacy of
both the pie-in-the-sky, and death-around-the-
corner legacies cannot be presumed corrected
merely because they are no longer openly preached.
They must be openly attacked. Have you ever asked
yourself how we got to be the favorite playthings of
death?  See the SNAPSHOT for 12 August.

## August 9

*The love of your woman should inspire you, not tire you.    —ali-*

# August 10

*When you demean your woman, you subject yourself to defeat.    –ali-*

Throughout the annals of times, at any point when any particular group of men have disrupted, disturbed or interrupted the established chain of nature, they have suffered for so doing. When man disrupts the balance of the food chain by wantonly killing animals for sport, he imperils himself by needlessly reducing his future stock of clothes and food. He subjects himself to death. When man disturbs the equilibrium of the ecology by deliberately destroying the trees, he imperils himself by exposing the risks of global warming. He subjects himself to death. There is a delicate balance in nature that must not be tampered with or destruction will follow. While it was left to other men to destroy the buffaloes and the rain forests, the black man has destroyed his woman! The results are no less remarkably infamous. The black man has imperiled himself through this reckless destruction and he has subjected himself to death. We have callously interrupted the flow of nature and have become the $1^{st}$ men in existence to demean, desert and to destroy our own women. No other men have ever done that kind of bullshit, so this is one lesson we did not learn from the white man! The southern belle was placed immediately upon a pedestal and a whole way of life sprung up out of the white man's desire to protect his queen. Study the history of this country and what you'll find is that the driving force behind most of the early laws was designed to protect the white woman. The lynchings and the murders of black men are potent reminders of this fact. Ain't it time to stop being fools?

## August 11

*If you simply use your existence as an act to take up space, then conditions will force you to make space for someone else.*          *–ali–*

When African-Americans specify definite reasons for our existence other than to breathe, then we'll move beyond being *"matter"*. (Remember from school what matter is? Something that has weight and takes up space.) (* We may not have made it into the history books, but there we are in science: *matter)* Among other peoples it is obviously well known that in order to thrive and prosper, there must exist a viable raison d'etre other than the common symptom of ingesting free air. Every people has their manifestos, their preambles, and their will to excellence. Still today, America gorges itself on its Manifest Destiny. Even the Blues Brothers claimed they were on a mission from God. On history's landscape, African-Americans are the rare exception. We claim no significance for our reason to be and our after-the-fact actions and conditions have been overly prototypical of being born merely to die. As long as our existence fails to meet the rigorous test of making us proud of whom we are, then there will never be any showing of advancement. Until such time, we will forever be viewed as the lesser included offense of America's Manifest Destiny (read: war crimes). It's time for the black man to stop being matter and to start to **matter!** Hold on sistas---we're coming.

## August 12

*He who convinces himself that the earth is an arena*
*for sport and play will one day have to reckon with*
*The Referee who knows the score.* —*ali*

The Quran teaches that the earth was created for just ends and that man was not created as a pasttime. This indicates that there is a divine purpose to man's being other than to merely exist as human ornaments of the earth. As for the black man, do you assume that it is our privilege to be the whipping boy of the universe? That is to be doubted. It's just that we have yet to exercise the power to find ourselves. We are enslaved because (1) the merits of our reason to be are in dispute, (2) the powers of self-determination are not supported by the history of our deeds, and (3) any facts that support our reason to be are either absent, not fully developed, or non-existent. If you think about it, that's just about the same reason why roaches and flies get killed. No one understands why they're here in the 1st place. *SPLAT1*
▪▪▪▪▪▪▪▪▪▪▪▪▪▪▪▪▪▪▪▪▪▪▪▪▪▪▪▪▪▪▪▪▪▪▪▪▪▪▪▪▪▪▪▪▪▪

# August 13

*The epitome of worthlessness is to have died without
experiencing the joy of living well. -ali-*

Does there exist any reliable evidence to support the probable accuracy of our death complex? In the same way that we, blacks, as a people, share a collective gene pool, we also share a collective consciousness. Our gene pool outfits us with certain physical traits and predispositions to specific diseases (such as sickle cell anemia). Well, our collective consciousness outfits us with shared mental traits and fears with the unalterable conclusion being that our future actions are the mental implications of assumed truths impinged upon our collective consciousness. Even though the punitive intent of our self-destructive behaviors is the resource of hereditary racism, our minds absorbed it as truth. Just as unborn infants feel their mother's fears and anxieties in the womb, we absorbed in our minds the impact of what we experienced via our senses. Now, let's go back and examine some immediate root causes that led us to a devaluation of our lives. Besides the brutal reality of slavery, it should be borne in mind that ½ of the Founding Fathers of this country were slaveowners and it was they who determined we were 3/5 of a man, the 1st legal imposition of our devaluation. The Supreme Court later decreed that a black man had no rights a white man was bound to respect. Our infant mortality rate is and has always been 10 times the rate as whites. Blacks who murder whites go to death row while the opposite is rare. All this data impinging upon our minds led us to unconsciously accept what superficially appeared as the reasoned and undeniable fact that our lives were not worth much in this country. This fact was articulated forcefully through our daily existence and it has remained uncontested until this day still. Only now it is a foregone conclusion that we verify. We sell ourselves cheap.

## August 14

*The ultimate foolishness of man is to deflate himself rather than to inflate himself. -ali-*

The only way for African-Americans to inflate the net worth of life is through love of self. Love is the framework within which it becomes vividly possible to appreciate the significance of our very substantial need to be overwhelmed by the beauty and joy of being. Our love of self must become so pronounced that it promotes all our longstanding perceptions, making them into tangible assets that we can use to negotiate the future. No limitations must be placed on our ability to love ourselves. We must learn.......be taught......know.........experience what its like to be swept away by love.

## August 15

*Do not be deceived. No man is that wise, strong, or powerful that he can disrupt, interrupt, or disturb his own nature without having to deal with the consequences. —ali*

-

   In the end, you must remember that there is really no better way to justify yourself than by loving yourself.   This is the simplest way to tune into nature.   Love yourself.   This is the shortest distance between you and peace.   This bonus is not reaped based upon the many clever ways you may imagine to love yourself, but rather in the strength of the love.   You need only to reach out to yourself. And then this is more or less the distance to paradise...

## August 16

*Good love is bright red lipstick for the soul.   –ali-*

What is suggested by the love of self is not the pompous aggrandizement of the body in name brand clothes, or lacquered nails or cool haircuts. The spectrum is not that superficial and your pampering would be better served if applied more internally. Still, however, the issue is not as much as how you love, but moreso with the serenity this love issues too you a return. Frequently, the flashy exponent of an exterior courtship only excuses you from appearing antisocial since keeping up with the Joneses will always award you plenty of company. In large part, you are simply applying makeup on your soul, and while you may look stunning, you have not nullified the unrest that is broadcast from within. The theory, in contrast, is to dress up the soul. It is a very low cost affair that will make your external self shine even when you're wearing your birthday suit.

## August 17

*Evolution will not be televised!*　　　　*-ali-*

In the early days of  *"It's all about me"*,  sistas abandoned the retreat of the household to join the revolution taking place in the streets.  Sistas operated with looseness untold of as Daisy Dukes and sexy pumps became the elegant wear of the nightclub set.  Sistas no longer dug being at the crib. They were wired for party and felt more or less the equal of any of the playas whom they felt were merely delivery boys of a wild, new lifestyle.  All of a sudden, sistas were ready to ride or die, to get down for theirs, and though this contradicted the rules of the game, but believe it or not, some sistas wanted to be in the driver's seat.  This notion was prompted, in small measure, by the fact that these women saw that money would come to whomever called it.  Once she saw chumps and suckas with paper, she was no longer content to be a trophy on someone's arm because she felt she could become a baller. By being small and petty, the brothas tipped their hands and the sistas concluded that anything a half a man could do-----a real woman could do better.

■■■■■■■■■■■■■■■■■■■■■■■■■■■■■■■■■■■■■■■■■■■

## August 18

## HOMEGIRL ANTHEM

*It 's all about me*
*C ause I'm dis and I'm dat*
*Don't be needing no nigga*
*When my pockets this phat*
*I wear designer shit*
*Cause I deserved it since birth*
*Be pushing a fly-assed Benzo*
*But dat's just a token of my worth*
*I got gold.  I got style*
*Damn, ain't I fine?*
*I got new nails and attitude*
*Well---the hair---it ain't mine*
*Still, just stare at my breasts*
*And the width of my hips*
*I know I'm all that, nigga*
*And a big bag of chips!*

## August 19

*Being "off the hook" will not get your ass off the hook.   —ali-*

African-American men have always been off the hook when it came to being in touch with their feelings. And now decades later, it appears that the sistas has gained ground in this pursuit of being soulfully valueless. It may be difficult to change. Due to the rapid deployment of our newly devised cultural practice of killing the men folk and abusing the females, there seems to be a valid need to remain and grow even colder and vicious. Non-feeling, for black folks, is a sort of invisible, wireless communication link between our public persona and our private fears. We have got to interfere with the disturbing conditions of the way we conduct our day to day affairs. This marginally suggests that each person should accept the responsibility for any bit of corruption he or she may have imposed upon his or her immediate home/street/community and then to take remedial steps to correct it.  This 'small grain' approach will afford us the freedom to see more clearly once some of the initial debris is removed and even though it may only reach door-to-door at first, the scale of the operation will expand under it's own moving forward.  A better home makes  a better block makes a better neighborhood  From there you just keep right on going/growing, touching lives with others who are doing the same thing.  In this way, our world will grow smaller and better.

## August 20
### *RESPECT EVERYTHING*

As time goes on, due to the structures in place, it will become more and more difficult to trust in love as healing. No matter how interested we may become in getting "racially" well, we will remain skeptical since even the most powerful remedy in the world won't gain much support if it is touted as snake oil. Universal love will never gather momentum as long as it is packaged as a finished product, a salary for time well-spent with someone else instead of as a mediator between the universe-at-large and your individual place in it. Universal love has an elementary system of operation: RESPECT EVERYTHING.

## August 21

*To deface nature will lead to environmental
blindness.   —ali—*

Given our long history of emotional deprivation on a national level, is it little wonder that the idea of universal love has failed to crystallize as a workable concept in our quest for freedom and identity?  This is because unlike our ancestors or our red brothers, the Native Americans, we do not view the land as a resource. Our contact and interaction with the land has always been ultimately destructive which has greatly contributed to our disregard for creation.  Technology has made us skeptics in the natural order of things as green parks decrease and parking lots increase.  The temptation to deface nature is a direct indicator of man's inner blindness.  The more assaults he launches against nature, the emptier he becomes inside.  It's a tragedy and a travesty.  Even though the dark man is not a major developer in this scheme against nature, we still must live amidst the wreckage and unfortunately for us the impending penalty will not be scaled down to reflect the degree of our non-participation.  It will be hell-to-pay for everyone.  As children of the sun, our fatally flawed affinity for the universe did not come into existence completely formed.  It was a learned response.  As such we can unlearn it.  And despite the fact that the quality of nature has been eroded, we can always seek kinship with the microcosm inside of us.  That's the advantage of being related to the universe. You are never far from home.

## August 22

*When you are in direct contact with the inner world, you will react and interact more purposefully with the outer world.*          *–ali–*

The approach to your inner world is relatively uncomplicated. Simply make contact. Your inner being cannot be controlled through weak, obscure commands. You must make contact. You must also direct your focus or else your energy will be dissipated. Even in the earliest stages of attempting contact, you must develop a systematic approach or else you will be relying on a free-wheeling hit-and-miss foray that will be too chaotic to produce the needed inner calm. Concentration and discipline are integral components of the process, but they will never intervene for you if you are not truly dedicated to reaching the core of your being. You will not get bigger muscles or a trimmer waistline. The goal is a peace-seeking mission. Peace with yourself. Peace with the universe. And it all starts within. You will not---never---be able to conquer the outer world until 1$^{st}$ you conquer the inner one. No ifs, ands, or buts about it. PEACE!

## August 23

*The lessons of soul are not meant to be pretty conversation pieces, propped up on the shelf of life. You must test and critique these lessons by walking them, not talking them. —ali-*

One thing that should make self-exploration and discovery so very appealing is that no matter who you are----no one is better suited to the task than you are!  Another attractive feature of getting to know yourself is that it still allows you the freedom to work on your outer self as well.  There is no competition between the selves.  As a matter of fact, they seek to mesh.  Union is encouraged.  But only at the pace and speed by which your individual *"coming 2 be"* can naturally benefit.  Your selves know best what will work and they will distribute results, expanding your knowledge of self is strict accordance with your ability to modify your life on the basis of what you've learned.  What is the benefit of having ready access to the natural means to calm yourself and not make use of this resource?  Why seek the pleasure of drugs when you understand how to naturally manipulate the brain's pleasure center for the release of endorphins (a natural high)?  It is indispensable that you realize that the philanthropic spirit of the inner shell *bestows* so that the outer shell *grows.*

## August 24

*Not knowing what "soul" is, is the greatest tragedy known to man.* —ali—

Though the soul is the final product of an ever-expansive divine-like consciousness, its temporal goal is to define a working link between all that is known in the universe and what it is precisely that you will need to know. In the end, it will remain this individualized knowledge that will have shaped and determined the course as well as the conditions of your life. This will be visibly expressed in the physical manner by which you estimate the characteristics of all that you may encounter during the course of your existence. The real goal is to do no harm on your way to becoming complete. Sad for us, but the primary nemesis is the conditioned labors of the western mind where instilled doctrines lurk that rent the selves asunder. The western mind was the first to embrace the separation. It separated church and state. It split off death from life. It divided the union of the mind and body; all unheard of heresies. And as if this wasn't enough, competition replaced cooperation, usurping it as a model of successful living. Thus was the foundation paved for strife and chaos? The church and the state had opposing agendas, death became a thing to be feared, and the mind manufactured sicknesses for the body. There was nothing cool about that. It stunted our growth. We are spiritual adolescents. Grow up. Don't be afraid to break the curfew of your inner oppression. In your soul, it is always safe after dark. Break free. Soar
■■■■■■■■■■■■■■■■■■■■■■■■■■■■■■■■■■■■■■■■■■■■■

## August 25

*Meditation is a spiritual pushup     -ali-*

Meditation is your spiritual elevator into the inner cosmos of your being.  It is a full-service provider, but with a single flaw.  It is not an all-at-once master-stroke.  Rather, it is a process of patiently taking one step at a time and with diligence, it will permit you to bridge the chasm between the selves, granting holistic (mental, spiritual, physical,) growth.  Meditation is not by any stretch of the imagination an up-front problem-solver.  Instead its function is more curative, helping to produce the benefits of natural healing that pave the way for the elimination of the stress that is the root cause of the problem.  In this it is coldly Darwinian and will offer you only the natural selection of the fittest solution to your problem---- the ability to think rationally and clearly.  In moments of crisis, immediate lucidity is your most potent ally.  It is only after you can see clearly that you can focus well enough to delegate yourself the authority to handle your biz'ness.

# August 26

*The death knell will knock you to your knees and make you kneel to the Creator.   -ali-*

Life is a spiritual exercise.  This, despite the fact that it is spent on a physical plane.  At the least, it will not be conditioned on how well you have fitted into the outer world, but the inner one.  On the approach of death, the worldly trinkets that one has spent so much time pursuing loses their luster.  Almost to a man, the intent is to get close to God or to reach inside to make peace with themselves.  At death, this need seems so crystal clear.  You suddenly understand that the security of your soul has been compromised and that it was your hectic lifestyle that had been the clear and present danger.  In the end, the slow down initiated by dying opens the fetters of your blindness and spotlights the fruit of your benign neglect. Usually, there is not much to be done to challenge the abuses, but death, just the same, acts somewhat as a remote sensing agent, allowing you to see clearly.  However, nothing compels you to wait until death opens your eyes.  The time is right now to act against the atrophy of the soul. Search for the peace within. Why not drop in to see what condition your condition is in.

## August 27

*When a people are oppressed, when one member of that group suffers, they all should yell "ouch"*

All during our sojourn in this country, African-Americans have had to narrow ourselves down by defining ourselves as victims and as such there was the real need to organize ourselves around established defenses. In general, our focus was shifted to reflect external realities and rabid enemies who seemed to be ubiquitous. This transformed us. In an effort to survive the risks, we became soulless cost-cutters, hoping to minimize the danger by shutting down on our role as managers of our destiny and settling for a niche as token survivalists. This broke with the ancient African tradition of being self-sufficient and once confronted with the threat of the loss of this time-honored practice, we lost access to our customized safety net: the capacity to train ourselves to conquer diversity. This loss was disastrous. We lost the foresight to see that what is done to one is done to all. Then our compassion for one another diminished and we took to sleeping with the enemy. The reality of divide and conquer rendered us both brain-dead and soul-damaged. We haven't recovered. And since we are no longer of one mind, we no longer address our real problems collectively. We're now too busy yelling "ouch" in different dialects.

# August 28

*Language is the audible component of a peoples'
ethical treatment of themselves.....-ali-*

The cerebral dissent of the black man's divorce from himself over the decades became more audible as the depletion of our love for each other has become glaringly pronounced. Even our greeting to one another has been symptomatic of the oncoming decline in the spiritual and physical rifts in the nature of our inter-tribal relationships. Witness the destruction. In the 70s, we affectionately addressed each other as  *"brothas"*. In the 80s, we started to drift and we acknowledged each other as *"cuz"*. At least we were still in the same family although not nearly as close. By the start of the 90s, we began the practice of addressing each other as *"friend"*. No longer related now, we moved farther away in our polarity until by midway the 90s we called each other "*dog!*  Hell, we're not even human to each other now. "DOG"! How in the world do a people go from being brothas to being dogs? Remember this: Rap (language) is the audible component of a peoples' ethical treatment of themselves. If they are living in a mental graveyard, you can't expect them to discourse on heavenly themes.
■■■■■■■■■■■■■■■■■■■■■■■■■■■■■■■■■■■■■■■■

## August 29

*Nothing is more instructive than pain.*          *–ali–*

Black collective failure is not defined by the presence or absence of a supposedly more superior, successful collective by which the inherent comparison is drawn. More or less, the failure is a sort or set of individualized instructions represented across the entire spectrum of the collective. These stifling calculations, standing alone and in isolation, track only the affected individuals, but however due to the dynamic manner by which information is executed sequentially, the performance of these instructions flow without resistance until an ensemble is created. With countless individual processors working together, the power of the instruction is maximized, triggering the same ennui   in the whole collective. At this point, the collective becomes an obstacle to itself and there is no longer a need to compute failure as a quality measurable against the gains of the larger, better evolved group. By now, the packaged instructions will engender itself to failure. If you want an example of this, you have to look no further than the recent spate of highly-placed black politicians who have gotten busted on corruption and ethics charges or the very visible black entertainers and athletes who commit senseless mistakes; it appears they fail when they have no reason to. Uh-oh. They can't escape the boogie. That's just how aggressive these instructions are. If you do not destroy the sequence code, the instruction to fail will execute itself no matter who you are----or where you go!
■■■■■■■■■■■■■■■■■■■■■■■■■■■■■■■■■■■■■■■■■■■■

## August 30

*In Amerikkka, prison is the posterchild of failure.*
*–ali–*

Another phenomenon that emerged out of this pattern is the present day prison system which has by and large supplanted the previous notions of failure as its own punishment. This has hinged on the foresight that technology would or could at some point merge failure into a viable industry. The possibility of this far-sighted idea was staggering. It had only to wait on technology to catch up. It has. And now the biz'ness of failure has a freshly-scrubbed face. At present, prison is one on the hottest growth industries in the country.

August 31

*A note to Black America*

Listen up.   Now dig this.   Black America
shamelessly treats prisoners as though we are the
premature, illegitimate bastards of the tribe and acts
as if we may never have any significant impact on
the conditions of the race as a whole.   However,
black America just may be mistaken. Believe it or
not, but it is we, the prisoners, who hold the keys
too many of the problems in our neighborhoods.
Right now, we hold many answers. Haven't you
ever considered why the white man won't help you
and you can't help yourselves. Neither of you know
how to address the issues properly. We prisoners
have a pretty good idea.  Who could possibly be in a
better position to dismantle and tear down the drug
trade in our neighborhoods than the ones who put it
in place to begin with?

## . September 1

*Accept who and what you are. Proudly.*     *-ali-*

Among any subjugated people, you will notice a phenomenon called "crossover disorder". It's a full-range condition that requires only a touch of vanity and/or self-hatred. The powerless employ it as a hopeful means of bolstering their impotence by adopting the "look" of those in power. These affected mannerisms and habits are foreign, alien or unnatural accessories that lean toward doing more damage to the self-esteem than providing any functional service. While there presently exist no truly measurable correlation between the high rate of "crossover disorder" prevalent among a people and the corresponding degree of the low self-esteem of that population, it is rampantly visible in the African-American community. It takes shape most noticeably in the guise of black women with blonde-dyed hair and blue contact lens, two common features of whites, and most unnatural to us. These customized features are alien too us as a tribe and matches nothing in our collective gene pool. These women have, in effect, produced a foreign reality that displays their disdain for their natural characteristics. The malady is likewise demonstrated by surgically altering your natural (collective) features (nose and lip reductions) to make you more compatible with a standard of beauty that is alien to your culture. If you somehow feel it is possible to escape who you are through this artificial pop-up window, it is not so. It is not an escape. It's only a license to look foolish...
■■■■■■■■■■■■■■■■■■■■■■■■■■■■■■■■■■■■■■■■■■■■

## September 2

*Crossing over to the other side is only another cross to bear.* —ali

-

The people depicted in yesterday's SNAPSHOT usually possess a particularly low capacity for appreciating their own culture. They are not strongly connected to the racial and genetic certainties of their identity so they opt to crossover in search of some imaginary, elusive expectation, if only a compliment. This, they relate as some type of achievement. No matter how exotic they may appear to be, they remain mutants and because of the existing patchwork of genetic impossibilities between the races, they risk both ostracism and ridicule. Regardless of who you are, you must verify your legitimacy by being yourself. There's no need to fake it. You can't. Even though your intentions are sincere, sooner or later you will have to revert back to form because contained within the way nature serviced you, there is a behavioral code made to fit your lifestyle. That's why no matter where you go, black folk always act the same: the walk, the talk, the slang, same name brand this or that. All around the world, we travel to the same eternal beat. And it's the same with other races. It's crystal clear that you may imitate them but you'll never be accepted because you can't dance to their genetic rhythm. Stay home. Didn't your Mama ever tell you not to be wandering off in strange places?

■■■■■■■■■■■■■■■■■■■■■■■■■■■■■■■■■■■■■■■■■■■■■■

## September 3

*Substantiate yourself. That's the best safeguard to prevent you from imitating someone else.   —ali-*

A key false assumption is this.  It is believed by many that in order to benefit from the example of a person that you must absorb his personality.  What is advocated as a model for success is that individual's life and not his lifestyle. So don't mistake that.   Since African-Americans are a highly visual people, meaning we tend to shape tangible truth out of what we see, we thereby shift our focus to the social dynamics of highly successful people's lifestyle instead of the more subtle influences that dictate their lives.  In copying the mannerisms of someone's life, we do not benefit and cannot be enriched by the values that mold and hold their lives in place.  Brothas want so much to be like Michael Jordan that they shave their heads and wear an earring to look like him physically. It is as if they feel they can acquire his skills through the maximization of his look. It does not work like that.  The potential lies within the terms of his life's values and not in the clothes or trinkets that power his lifestyle.  Blue eyes and blonde hair are genetic components peculiar to a people, but yet they are not the human behavior from which success evolved.  To get a clear view of how to follow in someone's footsteps, you must not aspire to join his personality cult.  What you're searching for is the intrinsic values that are the cornerstones of his success.  Forget the bald head or the earring.  Change your focus. Then you will gain ground...
■■■■■■■■■■■■■■■■■■■■■■■■■■■■■■■■■■■■■■■■■■■■■■■■■

# September 4

*Ain't nuthin' like a sista! This is the one thing I know to be true.   —ali—*

Bamboozled.   There's that word again.   Tricked. Hoodwinked.  That's what it means. And this time it applies to the sistas.  Black women have been pushed to the brink of this country's beauty standards, following every Eurocentric tip or hunch as to what it would take to make them perfect. Since the black woman has such a short historical attention span, she has missed the obvious beauty regimen:  *Just be yourself*.  For decades, they were stigmatized by the malicious rumor that their lips and butts were unattractive.  Instead of questioning the integrity of this racist gossip, they sought to make alterations on themselves.  It was so unnecessary.  Thank God that this fallacy was divested of its power; however sistas should have gotten a clue from the historical model of beauty that men of all continents hold up as the highest model of classic good looks----Nefertiti!  All civilized men of the world agree that her timeless beauty was flawless------and guess what, she was a sista!  If that wasn't enough, almost in the same breath, mention would be made of another great beauty---Cleopatra!  She too, most definitely, was a woman of color. And as if this was not enough, the gig really should have been up when white women, the so-assumed modern day standard-bearers of good looks felt physically vulnerable and decided to enhance themselves.  But what is it they did?  Made their lips and hips juicy and luscious just like the sistas.  The very exact things decried as unappealing was precisely what they desired: juicy lips and big butts.  Oh yeah, they like being dark too. That's why they tan.  See you were bamboozled. Get with the program. Just be yourself. *Do you!*

## September 5

*When there is nothing left to fear----fear failure.*
*–ali–*

Nothing was sacred any more once African-Americans lost the fear of failing their children. That was the final straw, the one that broke the camel's back. At the exact moment that we abandoned the capacity to struggle for the privilege of making the world more user-friendly to our offspring, we got trapped at a cosmic traffic stop, unable to proceed. But how did this grave disloyalty come to be? Evolution! Thanks to the way science, technology, and fads grow things, our children evolved into somewhat different creatures than us. There was a  cultural shift among them that influenced their value system into a mainstream cubbyhole that permitted them to scoff at even the things that had been fought for. The struggles and hard-won gains of the parents pushed the offspring into an early complacency, and after the 70s, the die was cast. The children obsessively believed they were party to equality since they drove the buses now, they went to good schools, and black people held political office. Our children no longer saw the big picture, They took a fancy instead to the small details of what  had been gained and then broke off into petty factions, arguing over those details, doing nuthin' more. They opted to wait on things to improve. Things got worse. This was a consequence of being of 2 minds. We no longer fear failing our children because our children feel there is nuthin' left to fear.

## September 6
*Riding someone's else jock-strap or skirt-tail is a quick trip to failure*

Another point to remember if you want to be successful is that in precisely the same way that our children do not label as important the same issues that we do, we must realize that what is important to other people does not necessarily have to matter to us. We must develop our own set of priorities and compel ourselves to cease torturing ourselves by specializing in taking the temperature of someone else's productivity. Nurture your own spirit because at any time when you are over-informed about another person's achievements, you are doing too many things at one time! You simply need to rest, recover, and get your own life. Hanging on to the rumors, reports or actual facts of someone else's progress is a good way to get transformed into a bad apple. You make it such a career of bothering other people's "get-up-and-go" that you appear incompetent and lazy. You effectively shortchange yourself by undermining your potential to do more and this sabotages the barometer of your day-to-day advances. Always remember that by riding someone else's jock-strap or skirt-tail is the well-behaved way to failure and the ultimate denial of seeking out those things that are of essential importance to you. Throughout the whole tenure of mankind, hitching your wagon to what is important to you as an individual has always enjoyed the good reputation of making one stand up and be counted.

## September 7

*Individual merit is simply a physical achievement going through the spin cycle of your mind.   –ali-*

The classic response to living "under the thunder" of someone else's success is to placate yourself by the misguided instruction that you're not getting left behind, but that the other person has a license to speed. Once you back this attitude up with the union of a low self-esteem and a flagging interest in self-improvement, this is appropriate behavior that underscores or highlights even your own importance to yourself. More than anything else, you demoralize yourself and faced with this sort of personal certification, no benefits are likely to accrue to you on the basis of what you feel you do or do not deserve. Sadly, good work habits cannot coexist alongside a sloppy attitude. Why? Because it mainly has to do with the reasonable assumption that concise action is the direct result of precise thinking. Individual merit is a physical process only after it has completed the spin cycle in your mind. Only then is it fluffed up with the tenure of achievement. You must establish credibility with yourself or the crippling nomination of someone else as your hero will remain intact and that's the status quo of a sucka. Wise up. Get involved in your own life. It's such a beautiful relationship.

# September 8

*A good school produces a good fool any time a student is not taught his own history.*

*-ali-*

Think about this. In this country, the instinct of bonding with someone else's success has such an easy spirit that it has become a type of national hobby. This attachment disorder is not viewed as the emotional deficit it is, but rather is elevated to cult status. Many people today are well-known, if not famous, not for anything they have done but more so because of the who they know. Name-dropping is more patriotic than the national anthem. This is a permanent feature of the gossip columnist or the entertainment critics who have transformed the phenomenon into high art. It's the same among all strata among African-Americans though the attachment disorder is not so flagrantly pronounced or proclaimed. What you must accept is that this is an internal power struggle created by an inherent need to be recognized and an incessant fear of not excelling. The compromise or cop-out is to undermine your chances of failure by attaching yourself to someone else's success. In the ghettoes and elsewhere, countless individuals are held in high esteem based on what their relatives did. This is merit on the family plan and due to its safety valve, many people never opt to leave its shadow. This parasitic cheating is a vicarious atonement for your moral ineptitude and as long as you allow this behavior to go unchecked, it will forever stall any chances you may have of standing on your own 2 feet because as long as you covet the role of being "the main man of the man" you will never rise above being someone who is good at tooting someone else's horn.

## September 9

*Hell on earth is the ultimate side-effect of being a fool.*       *–ali–*

To be good at what you do means knowing what to do when no one is watching. This insures that your personal integrity will never be reduced or trifled with. If your best behavior is only for public appearances, then your happy face is used solely as a magic bullet to fool an adoring public. So, what does your family get? Too many entertainers are guilty of this and they starve their households emotionally by shutting off their supply of love. But "stars" are not the only ones. It is equally true among corporate types and sanitation workers. Each must put on his/her "game" face and even for the duration of the work day, smile, grin, and placate others. This 2-faced role-playing is not healthy and it is an illness that you must be liberated from if there is a desire to improve the clarity of your living. You can always challenge the outcome of your relationship with the work world by reducing its impact upon you. A job is an economic pact between you and the marketplace, but when it extends beyond this reality, warning stickers should be applied. Your job is poised to take over your life. That's the dividends of the pursuit of success. It's like not reading the label on medication. You should beware of any side-effects of success and then make sure that you can take it home with you.

## September 10

*Before you can court success, you must learn how
to flirt with progress.  —ali-*

Uncover a hidden treasure.  Think of it as a well-kept secret...  De-identification is a managed-care concept that compels you to become an impartial, objective client in your own affairs.  It is the science of total detachment, the zen-like ability to conduct your personal biz'ness affairs as a surrogate persona.  In this way, you ignore the subjective emotionalism of the individual with the greatest influence in the matter-----you!  By effectively removing yourself from the vortex of your situation allows you increasing control due to your stance of objectivity?  Treating yourself as a business client is conscientious role-playing that may sometimes prove difficult but should never reflect upon your role as a consultant.  It is your job, under all circumstances, to render outstanding service to your clients through all the stages of the developing business relationship.  The key is to develop an early confidence in the relationship and then to communicate this confidence into an investment of prosperity.  Once you learn to misidentify, you will be able to ply the resultant objectivity into a viable assistance packet.  After all, the client did come with "instructions".  What you must do is to step back because sometimes you just have to get out of the way of your own progress.
■■■■■■■■■■■■■■■■■■■■■■■■■■■■■■■■■■■■■■■■■■■■■■■■

## September 11

*Until you learn to navigate your way safely on the information highway, your world will be a ghetto.*
*–ali–*

All the information you get from you about you can overwhelm you. When you process it in, it creates a progressive storehouse of random data by which you can evaluate who you are. However, the thoughts, memories, judgments, and biases can result in an abnormal prospective if these at-large combinations are not appraised in the mental environment from which they evolved. Failing to do so allows any disappointments, no matter how slight, to affect all other areas of your life, thus making it easier to accept that you are habitually flawed and that nothing good will ever come from anything you do. This negative thinking is easy to treat. The proven solution is for you to be specific about the origin of a set-back and then to restrict it to that environment. The fact that you did not do well in the gym should not paralyze what you do outside of the gym. The actions of the gym must be monitored within that sphere. Remember that information is a highway. Drive carefully. Don't get lost.

## September 12

*When you stand up to be counted, make sure that
your account with the devil is closed.  –ali*

Some African-Americans feel good knowing they have timid, hesitant values and opinions. These lead inevitably to their ongoing commitment to improper conduct.  And if that's not enough, they purchase the initiative to act so by losing enthusiasm for being the guardian of their individual actions. They volunteer to be led into the range of wrong conduct by not nurturing their priceless ability to develop strong principles. And in this age of anything goes, many feel assured that principles and scruples can get in the way of getting ahead.  They measure opportunity as the capacity to use others as a convenience or as a human bridge that keeps them from falling through the cracks. Under this pressure, their reaction is typically normal, but what is forgotten is that ugly behavior is a long-acting consequence that may not always be outlived and like all other life functions, ugly behavior produces waste as it gathers steam and one of the most damaging side-effects of this process is that you will continually re-engineer this behavior not realizing how devastating it is to your cycle of values.  You should remember that it is not possible to expand the life expectancy of your potential for success until you breathe life into your values.

## September 13

*Tame your demons.      –ali–*

If you have a history of dependency on actions that cause you problems and pain, that acquaint you with declining deterioration in your relationships, or that destabilize your life on a constant basis, then you need to (1) forego applying your actions as treatment to any situation affecting you that has occurred as a result of improper conduct, (2) not attempt any long-term solutions while under pressure, (3) watch for the efficiency of any short-term measures enacted, (4) not allow these so-called short-term solutions to exceed the limits of their effectiveness, and (5) not attempting to use any temporary benefits gained from these solutions as a substitute for seeking immediate outside assistance.. Thinking clearly has proven to be a safe and sure remedy, but it has also been demonstrated that even this won't produce the desired results if not followed up with even more clear thinking,

## September 13

*Tame your demons.*     *–ali-*

If you have a history of dependency on actions that cause you problems and pain, that acquaint you with declining deterioration in your relationships, or that destabilize your life on a constant basis, then you need to (1) forego applying your actions as treatment to any situation affecting you that has occurred as a result of improper conduct, (2) not attempt any long-term solutions while under pressure, (3) watch for the efficiency of any short-term measures enacted, (4) not allow these so-called short-term solutions to exceed the limits of their effectiveness, and (5) not attempting to use any temporary benefits gained from these solutions as a substitute for seeking immediate outside assistance.. Thinking clearly has proven to be a safe and sure remedy, but it has also been demonstrated that even this won't produce the desired results if not followed up with even more clear thinking,

# September 14

*In any crisis, **thinking** is always a great option!*
*-ali-*

African-Americans must learn how to affect realistic crisis resolution agendas. With persistence as a cornerstone of your treatment program, it may prove possible to stop or change your reliance on choices that spell disaster. As always THINKING provides less chance of going totally wrong since thought usually reduces the fear factor that prompts the attendant desperation that more times than not causes one to act without regard to reasoning. In most cases where there is an intense need for crisis resolution, it is the anticipation of what could happen that causes the fear, and usually we act upon our anticipation rather than anything more definitive. Sometimes after acting upon this initial assessment, re-assessment is difficult. So, it's full steam ahead------into disaster. Now, here are a few points to ponder. (1) In response to a problem, your hypersensitivity is a normal reaction to the problem, not the outcome or resolution of the problem! If not checked immediately after the introduction of the problem, this hypersensitivity becomes itself a liability that aggravates any attempt at the problem's resolution. Remember not to transfer the hype of the problem onto its resolution. (2) In every case, acting with extreme malice is cautioned against, (3) Space your approach to the problem. This is a safety valve that allows you to gauge responses and which serves as a yardstick to measure reactions. Much better than the sudden "all-or-nuthin' approach that leaves no doors open for options. (4) If things get worse, immediately try to determine if your actions contributed to the deteriorating situation or merely failed to relieve the deteriorating situation, and *(5) Persist in finding a solution.*

## September 15

### WHY???

For African-Americans, conflict/crisis resolution management is critical due to the class effects of violence among us. Successful conflict/crisis resolution has a high safety profile that has been adequately studied. When beginning a program of crisis management, those of us who expect short-term solutions must be cautioned that dependent upon circumstances, resolutions do not always concede to immediate cessation. Agreements and mutual accords sometimes have to be hammered out over time, but it is well worth the effort. As a people we must do what is necessary to contain the senseless class violence that is threatening to destroy us. Ask yourself this question. Why do we hate each other? WHY!?

## September 16

*Drama in your life is oftentimes a personal lecture
from your subconscious explaining to you the law
of cause and effect.        —ali—*

All too often, conflict is an individualized lecture
from your subconscious as a personal means to correct
the imbalance of your injustice to yourself.  It isn't
meant to become threatening to the point of peril or
jeopardy.  These flaws and defects in your personal
armor are not mere technicalities of your personality.
They are convictions requiring change.  Sometimes your
individual convictions exert adverse, disproportionate
influence over you when they are contacted by a change
and you feel the need to lash out.  It is rational to feel
hurt when you are faced with being wrong because it
hints that your search for relevance is irrelevant, but in
every instance, it is nothing more that your  personality
flirting with experience. At all points during your
existence, your principles must share duty with
experience, and conflict is the medium through which
the contact is effected. However there is no need for
situational trauma. Contact does not imply handpicked
conflict.  It simply means that your interests have
clashed with one another. Frequently, principles are a
quick roll of the dice affected by your gullibility at any
particular moment.  And this is oftentimes a poor
indicator of how hard to strike back. Sometimes, it is
only an appeal to relax and to listen.

## September 17

*Dig this. Your worldview is a premise. Your word is a promise. –ali–*

Normally, your viewpoint is being constantly re-structured because it represents and reflects (hopefully) new, improved guidelines for allowing you to live a more effective life. Your viewpoint is your expert personal monitor that can predict important changes in your lifestyle by the worldly functions that ages it. Years of wear and tear upon your viewpoint ages it, causing considerable damage to those aspects of your viewpoint that are inflexible. It is this chronic inflexibility that causes your worldview to break down in the face of on-going experience and change. This aging process gradually restricts your range of options because your viewpoint has deteriorated and needs a fitness program to whip it back into shape. With African-Americans males, this can be traumatic since we intimately associate our worldview with our "word'. In essence, we tailor our actions around our word no matter how problematic or short-sighted it may prove to be. It should be noted that your worldview is a premise; your word is a promise. Your worldview is a premise upon which you undertake actions to improve your lifestyle whereas your word is an IOU based upon the promise that things won't change

## September 18

*It's hard to view your worldview with your spiritual eye shut. —ali-*

Your quest for long-term survival will be based upon your viewpoint which when functioning smoothly is a "future shock" inhibitor. It boosts your capacity to handle and deal with the changes in opinions, fads or technologies that are yet to be sprung on you. A healthy viewpoint or worldview will absorb such innovations without harming itself or dimming your perspective. Commonly, your viewpoint is an organization of strongly(sometimes loosely) held beliefs, ideas, and conjectures that expand your horizons, acquainting you with new breakthroughs or that stymie your growth, introducing you to stagnation. All of your actions (not reactions) are composed of these viewpoints which normally divide themselves into ready-made, easy-to-access principles. Oftentimes, these principles represent a moral death sentence when your viewpoint is hitched to radical ideas that cannot fulfill your growth potential or when it is not possible to successfully "cut off" the spread of these ideas. None of us are that significant that we should find it necessary to make views other than our own unnecessary.

## September 19

*A bad habit is the oldest and best way to doom yourself to failure. —ali-*

Bear in mind that the oldest and best way to get your life in order is by weakening the hold of bad habits. Bad habits obstruct growth and prevent the stimulation of more productive things-to-do-with-your-life. Adding mental fatigue on top of a system of bad habits is a surefire method of traditional stress. A bad habit is a local, subconscious obscene "phone call" that travels through your brain, coaxing it and inducing your listening body to perform illicit acts upon itself. Mental timidity interferes with your ability to say no and once the bad habit is invested with the tenure of natural routine, it is propped up and sustained by the fear of withdrawal trauma... However, you can minimize the risk of a bad habit by limiting your exposure to any experience that inflames it...

## September 20

*Bad habits are simply vices under contract.    –ali-*

An individual will always sink to the level of his vices. Bad habits are simply vices under apprenticeship. The less determination in your life, the more the appetite for harmful, addictive behavior. While you can always spoon-feed yourself enough self-esteem to win against a vice, in most cases the addictive behavior is not placed under attack and this is what usually leads to the fragile infrastructure where bad habits and vices are bred. Pursuing this vice-by-vice approach to healing, you never will become healthy since your improvement will be evaluated by the feedback of your over-taxed self-worth. You can simplify the process by looking for ways to enhance your total behavioral perspective. Instead of using your self-esteem as a sort of mental time release capsule to attack individual bad habits on a one-on-one basis, you must attack the infrastructure as a whole. The piecemeal attempt at healing is nothing more that a useless placebo, the side effects of your fear of the vices themselves. Don't fear the fear. Search and destroy.

## September 21

*It's hard 2 feel good about yourself when you expect positive rewards from bad habits. —ali-*

Erecting a viable support system to immunize the inflammation of your behavior can be a big pay-off in your effort to control bad habits, but it doesn't stop there. The real reward comes when the level of your self-esteem has taken on the status of "watchdog", guarding you from habits that are impermissible or offensive to your evolving spirit. When your self-esteem becomes a fully self-service feel-good-about-yourself industry, the open account of bad habits won't generate any interest since enough positive information is distributed throughout your mental infrastructure so that nothing artificial is needed to stimulate or elate you. Just remember this. High self-esteem is the low cost of feeling good about yourself. Artificial stimulation can lead to a mental Chapter 11.

## September 22

*Self-love is the healing art of the soul. —ali-*

Self-love is the healing art of the soul. And the best thing that can be truthfully said of any other therapy is that it is only a distant second in therapeutic value to the love of self treatment. Everything affecting your well-being corresponds physically to the imbalances in your spirituality, and self-love naturally raises the level of the psychological desire to be whole. It is this ardent desire for wholeness (or Oneness) that is the ultimate source of relief as the enlightened organism will always reject that which will soil it.

## September 23

*Free your mind and your demons will flee.   –ali–*

Self-love feeds the soul.   It accomplishes this feat by balancing your need to be with the harmony of the universe.   Thus freed from undue stress, the liberated energy can then be used to exercise your reasonable pursuit of happiness. The ability to control your life with accurate assessments of your potential allows you to exert a well-defined resistance against internal uncertainty and stress. This permits you to manipulate external situations to your advantage without the wild speculations of despair and desperation that are the authors of most of the tension in your daily affairs.   By making yourself the recipient of your own love, you are more easily able to recycle and regenerate feelings of adequacy and then transfer them more effectively across the broad spectrum of your existence. Assisted by foresight, this feeling of adequacy will provide a continual link with every dimension of your behavior, verifying the ability of your spirit to make well-informed choices that regulate your life.

## September 24

*The best way to deal with stress is to act upon it before it acts upon you. –ali–*

Roughly speaking, stress, in principle, is energy trapped within a negative_frequency. Throughout the entire course of our lives, we perform according to the beat or frequency of our individual internal rhythm. This biological clock is forever ticking, emitting our personal energy with controlled, precise frequencies that are absolutely designed to suit the "timepiece" of our personal being. Stress or more aptly distress occurs when we permit circumstances to excite, slow or vary the field of our individual life frequency. The consequence is that once we become trapped outside the beat of our own rhythm, it is very likely that we stand still and it is this inertia that causes us to act out of character. We panic because the notion of existing at absolute zero compels us to do something----anything---to destroy the stress. What should be noted is that your response to distress is a reaction and under normal conditions, it is supremely better to act rather than to react.
■■■■■■■■■■■■■■■■■■■■■■■■■■■■■■■■■■■■■■■■■■■■

## September 25

*Distress is stress on steroids.  –ali-*

It is critical to understand the interrelationship of stress and distress.  This will allow a framework by which you can examine and observe the contractions of the one as it attempts synthesis with the other. Certain levels of stress are productive.  It is only when this energy is diverted, feeding negative input into the mechanism of your thoughts that it becomes distress.  You begin to suffer a character breakdown as you begin to identify with the imbalance instead of trying to restore the balance.  When confronted with distress, our first impulse is to move away from the center and attempt to fix the problem in a position off kilter from our strength.  We figure to correct the problem and then move back to center.  It would be better to maintain position and address it from our center.  Remember that it is not necessary to identify or verify distress by moving off balance to correct the imbalance.  This is not essential for relief. Whenever distress is triggered, maintain position, isolate the cause and then ATTACK!

## September 26

*Don't make orphans of your emotions until you accept that you are the father of them. —ali-*

African-American women are expert at what I call "emotional sequestering" which is what happens when adverse emotions are orphaned from their source. The attendant result is that the focus of the stress is shifted which provides an incentive to convert previously harmless situations into more emotionally volatile ones. When emotions are buried and sequestered, they expand rapidly, waiting to be exploited. This increase in emotional sensitivity enhances the prospects of a "flare-up", but the difficulty exists in that you will be on the wrong side of the incident. You will treat yourself as a victim when in effect, you are the instigator! By not dealing with an issue as it occurs, you put the stress where it does not belong, and by so doing, you become an advocate for an upcoming emotional confrontation. This trapped energy must be released and if you move it away from the surface of its true origin, you simply conserve it as reusable/renewable stress. African-American women, though well-versed in the art of emotional confrontation, must listen to flush out their emotions. This will allow them quicker recovery as the normal cycle for stress remains level. This will allow an immense contribution to their inner stability

## September 27

*Mental obesity will make your head fat and that ain't where it's at.  –Ali–*

Note this.  The pattern of similarity between the ways in which some people handle distress is proof enough of mental obesity. These individuals are "phat" in the head, meaning they do not know how to redistribute trapped energy throughout their head, so they respond to antagonistic stimuli by yelling, shouting, and temper tantrums. "Phat heads'" entire approach to stress management is to contain it until it explodes on its own volition.  For them, stress never provides enough information about its disruptive ability until it is full-blown distress at which time a temper tantrum sends a strong signal that the exposure level was unhealthy. Notwithstanding the weakness of "phat heads" to prevent their mental center from becoming subconscious "hot spots", they can learn to reduce their stress by not routinely experimenting with distress in large doses.  In theory, reduce the juice. Increase the peace.
■■■■■■■■■■■■■■■■■■■■■■■■■■■■■■■■■■■■■■■■

September 28

*The less the stress, the more the success.    —Ali-*

When stress escapes its protective loop, becoming distress, your body immediately becomes an armchair quarterback destined to handle the fumble.  If you are slow in tracking the origin of the distress back to its stressful roots, you will suffer more severely.   Distress will effect it strongest menace against you when you fail to identify the observable link between head "hurt" and body pain because  when it comes to what goes on inside your head, your body is a see-no-evil entity.  And this is one of the strangest of life's ironies because stress in the head can mean lumps on the ass.

September   29

*Distress is stress in excess.   –Ali-*

The trick is to learn what sacrifices to make. While it will never be possible to estimate the damage that will or could be induced by any stress, the effort should be to create a buffer so that stress does not increase to excess. Anything that disrupts the harmony of mind/body should not be undervalued, and techniques for the handling of such disharmony should be immediately put into effect. Don't wait on tangible consequences. The warnings should be proof enough. Look for ways to reduce the stress without delay. At that moment, though, the aim is not prognosis----but diagnosis. Recognition first. Then remedy. Oftentimes, the mistake is made to fix the problem without knowing what is exactly wrong. That's like taking the same pill for every ache. True, you must move quickly to dispel the stress, but it is always worthwhile to know beforehand what is bothering you. Why massage you leg when it is your arm that hurts?

## September 30

*Stress is not a plaything, so don't test drive it.*
*You'll only end up driving drunk.  −Ali−*

You score your 1$^{st}$ victory against stress when you realize you can't outsmart it.  And though you may train yourself in efficient ways to neutralize it, you will never actually "close the book" on stress because our traditional lifestyles mass produces it. The very best that can be done is to recognize how vulnerable we are and not provide such an available atmosphere for its residency.  When it occurs, we cannot become apocalyptic or fractured about it. Instead, we must reduce its impact and not allow it to mature.  Distress is a disease.  Vigilance impedes the velocity of stress, so stay tuned, stay focused, and stay prepared.

October 1

*Working knowledge*

*Wash hands of all bullshit
*Do not accede to being merely a face in the crowd
*Whenever possible-------exert influence
*Don't isolate yourself or target yourself for
mediocrity
*Familiarize yourself with what is going on
*TAKE CHARGE!!!

## October 2

*Good news for the Hip-Hop Nation*

The problem with some of today's youth is that they have no way to determine the threshold of their ability. They lack concrete data on the nature of how to fit into a society that seems to go in too many directions at once. Easily disillusioned, youth has become a global society unto itself, often offering dramatic resistance to any feature of life that falls outside the vicinity of glamour or guns. Susceptible to paranoia, they feel the world is out to eliminate them, so only selective contact is viewed as wholesome. This looming threat of insensitivity will continue to affect the terms of the generation gap adversely. Regardless of what moniker is used to depict this situation, it should be called "messing wit' the kids". In practice, children today are bred. They live blamelessly in an environment that commercially alters them, improving their impotency and inability to adjust to a world where rule changes are the only constant. This essentially eliminates conformity. Regardless of how today's youth acquire their values, they will be promoted with the emphasis on survival. This is not seen as self-defeating. It is viewed as a contribution to the undoing of society at-large.

## October 3

*The black nation does not need yes-men. It needs men!    -ali-*

The protest of the hip-hop nation against yesterday's values is routine house-cleaning. It is their rebel yell. They do not desire the chance to proliferate and grow into the yes-men of tomorrow. They refuse to become the new agents of black conformity to a system that will deny them either a hand or toe-hold. They exist in a world where everyone is classed into 2 very distinct groups; homeboys or interlopers. The selection process is obvious. You are either down or you're not. Choose sides.

■■■■■■■■■■■■■■■■■■■■■■■■■■■■■■■■■■■■■■■■■■■■

## October 4

*One sure way to get ahead is to stay ahead of the bullshit.  –ali–*

Oftentimes one generation will pass on the spirit of resistance to another by providing them useful information or examples.  In addition, the elders will occasionally take it upon themselves to lead the charge into the heart of the struggle, but for the hip-hop nation this did not happen.  They were not integrated into their Moms' and Pops' struggle for equality or justice.  In fact, they were not even offered protection from the enemies of equality and justice.  In a sad twist of fate, they were left unguarded in a hostile environment. Those lucky enough to survive learned of their elders' betrayal and are now urban guerrillas seeking to limit the expansion of their parents' dismal legacy while simultaneously fighting the powers that be.  There is no chicken soup for the soul of the oppressed and so the only logical solution for the hip-hop nation is to bring on the noize!

October 5

*Empowerment is a magic trick that allows you to turn your father's noose into a loophole that will grant you the luxury to wiggle your way out of poverty. —ali*

The hip-hop nation's most important psychological loophole is that you are under no morally binding requirement to follow the ways of your fathers. Your 1st victory is that you are still able to participate in life despite the stunning failure of your parents. You must capitalize on this historic opportunity by warming up your ideas and by not squandering your ability to negotiate from a position of strength. You must be heartened by the clear-cut logic that you can develop alternative choices to the expansive defeats allowed by those before you. Choose efficiency over the advocacy of remaining passive in the face of the status quo. Explore your individual role in tackling the enormous challenges that expose the race to extinction, and then give your full support to saving us!

## October 6

*In the hood, you will starve as quickly on a bad idea
as you will from wishful thinking.  —ali-*

The hip-hop nation must forever keep in mind
that passivity is a non-deductible contribution to a
bad idea. You cannot wait   on either congressional
or parental approval to survive. You must take,
unaided, the remarkable 1st step towards erasing the
objections that you are a "throw-away" people.
Significant pending proposals aggressively promote
your doom. Eliminating you is the obvious expense
of doing biz'ness in a country where you are the key
public nuisance and   there will never be any peace
accords between Washington and the Hip-Hop
nation because the demonstrated antagonism of the
one against the other will serve to hinder that
process.  As long as you do not beg for permission
to exist, you will continuously be in regular contact
with the fire power of the powers that be**. RESIST**!

## October 7

*If you ain't hard enough to take it to the limit, then do yourself a favor by not stepping off your front porch.* —ali

-

Taking it to the limit is the "inheritance tax" incurred by taking that remarkable 1st step. Action now turns inward where solidarity plays a pivotal role in deciding the course of action against he troubles inherited from your fathers. Raise the roof and ignore the background voices of the elders who are or were the allies and yes-men of the enemy. Their weak cries are noize pollution. Stamp out noize pollution. Ist things 1st!

■■■■■■■■■■■■■■■■■■■■■■■■■■■■■■■■■■■■■■■■■■■■■■■■

## October 8

*Whenever the playing field is uneven, defeat and
failure are always the pom-pom girls. –ali-*

There are no new ways to fight back on an
uneven playing field. The disadvantage is a well-
disguised, well-devised ploy of the powerful
employed to circumvent your progress. It
undermines your confidence and its impact is to
compel you to negotiate unreasonable terms that
will stunt not only your immediate chances of
survival, but also to disrupt your future capacity to
resist. **BEWARE**!

October 9

*Address the mess.    –ali-*

You (Hip-Hop Nation) cannot overlook your critical role in the existence of the race. If you insist on doing little more than the bare minimum, then you too will arm your offspring with an attitude that will imperil their survival. You must take stronger steps than your fathers did. Your campaign must develop a closer relationship with tactics and strategies than ever before. If you fail to account for your full collective potential then you will taint the impact of YOUR struggle. Everything must be overseen. Nothing can be overlooked. Everyone must strive in unison to reverse the trend of our national defeat. **<u>ADDRESS THE MESS!</u>**

## October 10

*You gotta make shit happen because tomorrow
never comes to those who wait.  –ali–*

Knowing that you are under attack and then not moving vigorously to repel that attack underscores a policy of stupidity.    Subsidized racism has announced itself loudly. Institutionalized bias has made itself clear.  Other forms of discrimination are daily features of your routine lives.  What more do you need?   When do you fight back?   What if tomorrow never comes?!  **NOW IS THE TIME**.

## October 11

*A fool is always someone's meal ticket.  –ali-*

You will not spot the Deliverer.  And waiting on someone to hand deliver you to success should never be the mandate of a people or person whose history has demonstrated that such a  'lookout" is fundamentally unsound.  The only strategy that can result from such an approach is certified disaster. Waiting, or standing still, when your head is in the lion's mouth only encourages more lions, and this can never be construed as a step in the right direction.  Roughly speaking, what it does construe is that everyone will die!  Abandon this stupid policy.  Don't provide free meals for the lions.

## October 12

*Equality now. Superiority later. –ali-*

You must act at once to announce a no-compromise policy against the world. Your current agenda must be to make it good and damn clear that for the moment you will accept full equality. *(Your children and their children's duty will be to push for superiority) Presently, however, you must press this idea of equality into your music. Your movies. Your individual lifestyles. The remainder of your energy should then go to convening under a single banner. This way, you evade the major threat of disunity by the age-old implementation of divide-and-conquer. While uniting under the stewardship of UNITY, there should be an interim management program that makes sure no one gets lost or left behind along the way to the nation-building, and that everyone will be able to get in where they best fit in.

■■■■■■■■■■■■■■■■■■■■■■■■■■■■■■■■■■■■■■■■■■■

## October 13

*Beware of proclaiming the claims of the ol' heads who wanna do shit now that they should have done a long time ago.   –ali-*

In times of conflict, you must ignore the initiative to purchase the advice of "ol' heads" that all at once get reborn. They may be out to launch a counter-revolution. Work closely with those who genuinely share your interests, but 1$^{st}$ investigate the claims they proclaim. One well-managed merger with a spy and your march will become a farce. Your struggle will become a tussle, and your light will fade to night.

## October 14

*Ain't no distinction in extinction.   –ali-*

Teach your children well!  The Hip-Hop Nation is the final buffer between us and extinction.  If you fail to produce smart children, then there will be no other renewable sources of strength for us as a people.  Another generation of junkies and jail-prone youth will finish us off.  We are already overpopulated with members of the race who play no vital function in our right to exist.  This is illustrated by the correlation between our high infant mortality rate and our high prison population. These important sources of our human resources do not serve us and that which does not serve you, paves your way to destruction.

October 15

*Knowledge is a power tool for your head.  —ali*

A proper education is like shopping for power tools for your head.  Ignorance on the other hand offers no compensation for the losses incurred by its use.  And while ignorance is freely dispensed on the open market, education must be sought.  Ignorance will lure you.  Education will elude you. In the eclectic mix of available data and info in today's world, you can positively identify education by the fact that when it competes with ignorance, education will be the dirtiest of the two

October 16

*Ignorance is the Head-Start of slaves.  –ali-*

Powerless black men are the unbidden, though savvy, marketing agent of ignorance.  Their ignorance has caused greater harm to our children than any environmental or external threat because our children have suffered more disproportionately from this lack of guidance and leadership than from anything else in combination.  The Hip-Hop Nation must forego the paths of ignorance trod by their fathers and not only recommend change, but to initiate it.  The commercial learning of our children must be supplemented by education that prepares them for leadership roles.  They cannot subsist on information that trains them for mediocrity or which awards them for complacency.  Act now to end education that produces slaves.

October 17

*Bling-Bling without consciousness is 'designer' slavery.* –ali-

The Hip-hop Nation must be on the steering committee to phase out *"designer slavery"*. You must rev up the institution of doing biz'ness with yourselves and to stamp out the enchantment with designers who prefer your servitude rather than your business. Once you identify yourself as the viable market you are, then you will be available to protect your assets by circulating money through the Nation so that it is not just fondled by black hands but funneled into black causes. This will be a clear sign of your arrival in the financial mainstream.
■■■■■■■■■■■■■■■■■■■■■■■■■■■■■■■■■■■■■■■■■

## October 18

*Niggaz who merely wait on the next day to come without planning for that day are usually the niggaz waiting on a casket and 6 feet of dirt.  —ali-*

Enormous amounts of cash have been spent to construct new wildlife preserves for the Hip-Hop nation. They are called prisons!  And given the tight rein of discrimination, these preserves are proving triumphant in bartering with your lives.  Jailees are in the same sinking boat as junkies.  They are of no use to the cause. You shouldn't have to convince yourselves of the virtue of this type of predicament. It depletes your forces.  It will have a profound effect on how much you can expand and in many cases, how quickly you will fail.  All human resources must be maintained.  This is the brainchild of necessity...
■■■■■■■■■■■■■■■■■■■■■■■■■■■■■■■■■■■■■■■■■■■

## October 19

*For the black man in America, prisons are either a womb or a tomb. They will either nurture you so you will keep coming back, or they will kill so you can't come back. —ali-*

Biz'ness as usual cannot be set as a fair price for the existence of the Hip-Hop nation. You cannot remain detached, isolated or neutral in the provisions of your future. In a historical context, you must gain popularity by claiming credit for the ribbon-cutting ceremony that ends your servitude to the ways things are supposed to be. It is your inherited prerogative to show no favoritism to recreational tokenism. Strike no deals with either the rhetoric or reality of failure. Don't make bids for your freedom by stuffing your pockets with petty acquisitions, positions, or appropriations. Care less about what they think of you. Care more about what you think of yourself. Will you still respect yourself in the morning?

October 20

*The inherited prerogative of the Hip-Hop Nation*
*must be to strike no deals with failure. –ali-*

Your culture is the most diverse ever and through the advances of science and technology, the one farthest behind. Due to this failure to compete, you have been pushed back to the jungle's edge despite the fact of your fashionably correct attire. Your lock-and-key relationship with technology will crudely hamper your capacity to link up your alliances, and your initial attempts to affect public policy, but you must take those risks. You must learn to watch out for all the processes of disruption that will be used against you. The most prevalent one being the theory of your incompetence. Everything you attempt will be measured against the scale of this theory. You must refute it with excellence. Anything less would be gambling with any real contribution that you could make. It must be recognized that we are so far behind that our general resentment will no longer pass as an effective remedy against our losses. The only remedy is to win.

## October 21

*Prayer does not stop war.  –ali-*

This is no abstract notion.  You (Hip-Hop Nation) come from broken homes where many of your parents were estranged from the ruthless reality of a war going on. Even though they could hear the bombs being dropped, they simply prayed that everything would go away.  They were defrauded by tokenism and then generally ignored. After this, their chronicle of resistance became a nationally renowned song-and-dance performance attended to by politicians whose relationship with change had never been close.  The celebration of the Hip-Hop Nation must begin by the building of a new home where the independence of the race may reside.  No more songs-and-dances.  No more back-door entrances.  No more feigned sympathy. **Success**. That's the word of the day. **Success**. That's what it's all about.  **Success**.

## October 22

*Winning is the only remedy for what ails the black man. —ali-*

Don't do drugs! Being on drugs will weaken your case for being taken and treated seriously. History will judge you severely if you employ your resources and brainpower solely to buy or sell dope instead of directing it to coax every tomorrow into becoming a less naughty place to enter. Waiting simply for the next day is akin to begging life for crumbs when she does not mind sharing the whole loaf.
■■■■■■■■■■■■■■■■■■■■■■■■■■■■■■■■■■■■■■■■■■■■

## October 23

*You don't have to mourn the morning after when you've made all the right moves the night before. –*
*ali-*

The coming out party for the Hip-hop Nation will be the largest operation in our collective history. It will signal an end to the horror of our "times of mourning". No more dazzling disappointments of defeats. You (Hip-Hop Nation) must display your intrinsic affinity to disrupt the status quo of our demoralizing conditions, and order a delay to our collective bargaining with the influential dynamics of soup line bullshit. You must lose no opportunity to withdraw from the strategic laxity of our past tragedies and issue a new, fully functioning agenda. You must not be swayed by any outsiders claiming a special relationship with us, via whatever source or authority. It is time to DO FOR SELF. That means the Hip-Hop Nation must be filled with doers!

■■■■■■■■■■■■■■■■■■■■■■■■■■■■■■■■■■■■■■■■■

## October 24

*To get there from here---**GO HARD!!!***

Your determination to succeed is the most viable, visible sign of security you will receive during the period of struggling to get there from here. You cannot depend on early rumor or last hour resolutions. Stay the course. You possess a strong solid objective: **FREEDOM**. Nothing else compares to it so there is no mistaking it and no one should be able to fool you about it. You will know it when you possess it. Until then, you must strive for it. We have passed too much time as slaves and servants. Our general pain and common enemies have not lessened. To your task, Hip-Hop Nation!

**GO HARD!**

## October 25

*One of the greatest conversion known to man is that*
*of going from a slave to a free man.* —ali-
When you look deeper into the conversion process
of becoming free, it is not enough to assume that
one is born free. He must live free!

## October26

*Being aware of where you fit in will take the
mystery out of trying to buy time from life.* —ali-

A fact that cannot be ignored or overlooked is
that if the Hip-Hop Nation is not aware of the past,
their ignorance will be like sending a resume to the
devil. Knowing your history is on-the-job training
for success. Get rooted.
■■■■■■■■■■■■■■■■■■■■■■■■■■■■■■■■■■■■■■■■■

October 27

*Get used to it. In the hood, you don't commune*
*with nature or soak up sunsets. You fight to survive.*
*–ali-*

The Hip-Hop Nation must develop a passion 4 inventing a totally new communications network where we control our own collective image because as long as others decide what we look like in the media, we will remain impotent in our ability to influence what the world thinks of us.
■■■■■■■■■■■■■■■■■■■■■■■■■■■■■■■■■■■■■■■■■

## October 28

*In the hood, where compromise is never a possibility or a reality, you gotta pay for your learning.  —ali-*

Though the hood may have been the environment where your life began, that doesn't mean it has to be the place where it ends. You must be brave enough to explore the culture beyond the hood and then make it friendly to you. However, one thing you must remember is that the white world will not tuck you in at night or give you milk and cookies when you're ill, so you must stop believing that holding your hand out for help is a winning formula. Here's what I suggest. Get a game plan and follow it. After all, this is your life. You can imagine it to be this or that, but it ain't. It's a war zone where any amenities you gain today probably won't mean shit tomorrow. In the hood, you pay as you go, but just where is it you're going? Church, jail, or hell.?

## October 29

*Without an inventory of success, it is easy to accept failure as a norm.* –ali-

You can't move by standing still. And in the hood, one of the major things you need to stack paper is momentum. Without momentum, you stand still. Even if you are foolish enough to believe in the hoped-for experience of being in the right place at the right time, even that ain't likely to happen if you standing still. So move. Get it on. Lean back and flex your muscles. Then make shit happen.

October 30

*There is a big difference between confidence and arrogance. Confidence will show you luv. Arrogance will get you killed.* –ali-

Despite all the negatives, there  can be some good in the hood, but first you must stop complaining and blaming others, God included, for your failures. You must invent a new YOU. This means you must transform your actions and reactions, and be realistic about your ambitions. The hood ain't gonna let you front, so the usual stunts won't work. You need a brand new bag of *fundamentals.* Why? Because you must "*fund da mental*" aspects of your life before you can fuel the physical ones.

October 31

*The hood is the world's School Of Hard Knocks.*
*—ali—*

You might as well hear this. The only ghosts and goblins we need fear are the ones generated from the negative energy of our past mistakes. And while we still may not possess anything close to a perfect solution, the Hip-Hop Nation is in no position to give up the search. You have got to keep on looking as long as there are monsters under our beds.

■■■■■■■■■■■■■■■■■■■■■■■■■■■■■■■■■■■■■■■■■■■■

## November 1

*Once you enrich yourself with power, it becomes much easier to take advantage of opportunities that permit you to distance yourself from failure.* —ali—

**Empowerment.** That's what (you) black woman must concern yourself with. To opt for less is a moral sanction against yourself since you have the responsibility to conduct all your affairs under the watchful eye of this concept. **Empowerment.** You cannot operate successfully without it or maintain any real distance between the pain of defeat and the worship of failure. It is especially important for you, black woman, to take advantage of every opportunity to enrich yourself with power, and then use it to schedule all the activities of your life---- from the boardroom to the bedroom. This allows you the authority to prohibit and suspend all the conditions of your prior intoxication with powerlessness. It's a Slim-Fast diet for success

.

## November 2

### FYI

Do you really know who the black woman is?! Well, she comes in 34 different shades and that's more flava than Baskins-Robbins. Her majesty has been hailed as supreme throughout all of recorded history, and her beauty is the divine acknowledgement of what God can do when He wants to show off. When God created the black woman, He spared none of His wonderful magic, withheld none of His Infinite Wisdom, and denied her none of His secrets. He borrowed the sparkle from the sun and gave it too her to wear as a smile. He invested her laughter with a beauty that surpassed the melody of the birds. He made her personality as colorful as the rainbow, her touch as soft as a gentle breeze, and her love as precious as gold. And that's who the black woman is--------- Just so you'd know.

## November 3

*Arousal is an aphrodisiac that controls men's behavior. –ali–*

**Entitlement.** This is exactly what *pussy power* provides for black women   It entitles them specifically to the exclusive attention of black men who need only be told what to do in order not to lose the   privilege of sex.   One of the natural conditions arising from the power of sex is the inherent ability to modify and fashion behavior, for contained within the capacity to arouse the male is the corresponding ability to cause him to conform. The mere threat of a punitive measure of this severity will evoke a definite change in the black man, and through the agency of this single threat, the black woman can decidedly interfere and disrupt the penchant of the black man to accept things "as is".  On a collective level, the only power the black man can lay claim to is that of his sexual prowess. Deny him this and watch the brothas snap to attention.  You, black woman, have the power to influence and induce change in the way things go. Make warriors out of your men and then send them out to bring you back the world for your playground. Use your power.  You can never use it up.

## November 4

*Knowing who you are gives others permission to speak about you behind your back and realize it's the same thing they would say to your face.  —ali-*

Knowing who you are is the ultimate passport. Awareness and recognition of your strengths allows you to participate in effectively promoting yourself and articulating your needs.  This elevates you to a plateau where you act as a pioneer in your own growth and development  without compromising your integrity.  The willingness of others to support you should not be viewed as a sponsorship for ego-mismanagement, but rather must be taken as a pre-existing case for your own personal validation.  This is a positive, so  you must use this triumph as a point of pride so that it can motivate others to come into their own.  The dynamics of receiving help is the most incredibly dynamic reason to offer it to others. Never forget that.

## November 5

*Friction between the pursuit of happiness and the*
*easy availability of misery is no fiction.    –ali–*

Who goes there?!  One of the can't-be-helped components of emancipation is that it automatically makes you the new kid on the block.  Before you go any further, understand that this  status confers you nothing!  It  merely implies that you must collect a group of "professional" advisors, mainly your *heart* and your *head* to show you how to pursue this newly-acquired lifestyle with the minimum amount of sacrifice.  You  offer yourself a good shot at personalized longevity if you make a careful study of both the strengths and weaknesses of your head and heart. Mental resources must be employed so that the short-term objectives of your head do not infringe upon the long-term objectives of your heart.  You must formulate a conscious plan to wed this diversity together so that what you allow in your head is as  easy an alliance of who you let into your heart.  You must always remember that the residual friction caused by an imbalance in your long-term and short-term goals is the raw material that is the essence of permanent failure

## November 6

*When goodbye mean gone-----You should always
shut the door on your way out.     —ali-*

Today, originate a goodbye rite of passage to your old self and see her off without a lot of crying and sadness. Crying over the fact that you're finally parting ways with a negative attitude only reinforces the idea that foolishness has a certain appeal too you. It will be especially beneficial if you attempt to make sense of the terms of your departure and the very first assessment you must make is that you are never coming back! So from wherever you part---the head or the heart, the rest of you must be fully advised that after goodbye, hello "again" can never be an option. You are gone. Now, with all this unused space left from the divorce of negative and ineffective thinking and living, you must elevate your standards of deciding what is best for you. Do not erect "sidelines" or else you may become tempted to become a spectator, watching events present themselves too you. Instead, permit things to occur only on the playing field of your choice where it is you who decides whether to prioritize or to simplify. Once you learn to balance your current needs with the demands of your future, you will recognize how to push back failure. In such cases, parting is so sweet.

## November 7

*In order to become effective, you first must destroy the effects of being of no effect.  —ali-*

**BEWARE!!!**  Women of color have a shared mental history of forgetfulness which has proven to be a clear benefit to their detractors, so you are urged, encouraged, and advised to always recall the effects of being of no effect!   Know that being effective is  a learned skill and that it is  has to be cultivated   and   kept   in   good   working   order. Unproductivity will not stay away without careful planning on your part and you can never rule out the possibility of being enslaved again because the enemies of your emancipation will forever retain some degree of power.  They know you. They have marketed your weaknesses. They will miss you. Remember that it is not in keeping with good slave-masters, whether internal or external, to simply let you escape, so you must minimize the risks of recapture. THINKING always allows you to stay 2 steps ahead of who's chasing you.

## November 8

*.In your race to freedom, sometimes it is not how fast or how far you run----but how soon. –ali-*

Just so you'd know. Emancipation, unfortunately, does provide some measure of risk. This is the actual contrast between what you visibly knew and experienced as a loser, and the unknown long-term effects of what will be. A similar fear always exists when familiarity is being abandoned, and the intensity is directly related to how long and how deeply you were associated with the illness of not being yourself. Trust this: There are no conflicting reports. ***FREEDOM IS BETTER THAN SLAVERY.*** And nothing has greater potential. Emancipate yourself.

## November 9

*It is easier to live with your faults when you love
yourself enough o recognize them.   –ali–*

Enjoy success!  That's what it's for. Success not
only highlights the caliber of your existence, it also
endorses your unfathomable belief in your
character. Don't be a spoil-sport by enduring
success in silence. Why should you  not be proud
when success is the eloquent supporter of you right-
to-be. There is nothing cavalier about pulling
yourself  up by your own bootstraps.  In fact, it is
the  singular, most accomplished thing you can do
with your existence, and while at times, it may not
be easy, the road to success will always be smoother
if you conscientiously follow the day-to-day
management program of loving yourself.

## November 10

### *A Woman's Place*

A woman's place ain't in no kitchen
Rattling no pots and pans
Neither is it in the bedroom
Laid down beside some lazy man
A woman's thang  ain't  birthin' babies
Or watching soaps all day
And it damn sho' ain't at the beauty shop
Or on her knees to stay
A woman's place is in the thick of things
Bringing 'girlpower' to the table
'Cause the same hand that's gonna rock the world
Got strong from rocking the cradle

## November 11

*Just 'cause you can see 'em doesn't mean you can catch 'em. —ali-*

To court lasting success in the corporate world, you cannot forget about racism or sexism. You must refocus. You have gone from one level to another and the demographics may have changed, but racism and sexism have been more thoroughly disguised, so you might mistake them in formal attire. The iron curtain of the welfare system is now the glass ceiling of the marketplace, and while glass does offer a view, it is still oppressive.

## November 12

*Pride is being grateful that God made you-----YOU.*
*–ali–*

Doing yourself proud is the greatest experiment in the world of any of us. You will have your ups and downs, and you will observe you share of heartache and disappointment, but you must high-five yourself by sticking with the program and standing up for your belief in you. As always, remember that when you are out from under the head-lock of world opinion and under the momentum of your own drive and determination that all you truly need is the persistence to keep moving. That's good ol', down-home inspiration. No substitute has ever been found for it. Use it as you must.

## November 13

*On the journey to freedom—go 1$^{st}$ class.      - ali-*

One terrific thing about freedom is that it awards you the liberty to pick and choose your own battles. You are no longer a helpless victim, so you can wait on the right moment to "get even", but you must restrain yourself from battling for the sake of battling because doing so will allow you to swerve from your initial goals. You should always bear in mind that oppression is offensive to freedom so don't get smothered by the psychological urge to pay others back in full. That's a journey down a dead end street. Fight 'cause you've got a cause.

## November 14

*A goal simply tells you to go-all out for what goads you on.     –ali–*

It's all about goals.  They are what makes each journey distinct and worthwhile. Goals prevent you from sleeping at the wheel as well as from sleeping in the wrong beds.  Your goals are the pot of gold at the rainbow's end.  They are your exclusive  life-shaping, cosmic, made-for-self cheering section. If you nurture and pamper them, they will watch your back.

## November 15

O Black Woman!

Compelling the black man to bring you the world is the appropriate response to your desires. At no point of time during our historical perspective in this country were you ever absent from him, and you witnessed up-close and personal what the feats of his mighty labor could produce. You were an eyewitness, had a bird's eye view of what the black man as a slave wrought for the white man. He can be made to do it again, but this time for you! Withhold the booty and get ready to get hooked up. Without a doubt, niggas will look out for the cook-out.

November 16

*If things get better a time goes along, shouldn't we be in paradise by now.* —ali-

You, black woman, must forfeit the unearned notion that the world will get better as time passes. This type of thinking means that you will take no action to improve your own conditions. Sadly, your passivity specifies that your joy will either be limited or withheld totally because you cannot delegate time to act by proxy. Now is the moment for sistas to make themselves eligible for duty. Your reliance upon the wholesale acceptance of universal acts of charity are all procedural requirements that only vests you with the live testimony of your defeatist attitude. You have the responsibility to make use of your life in a manner consistent with interests that demonstrate your total independence from the watching out and waiting for things to happen. You must seize the day---- and make shit happen. EXHALE.

## November 17

*Never trust that anyone is who they say they are.  –
ali-*

A sista's groove is that of all the people on the planet, she possesses the most  idealized concept of the white man as a savior-in-waiting.. For the older sista, it's  Jesus.  To the sista in the projects, it's Uncle Sam and his 1st of the month welfare check; and to the young sista, it's Santa Claus. Better get hip, girl. You have been a burden to carry, and the white man ain't trying to rescue you, he trying to lay your ass down!

## November 18

*Whenever you can't see it coming, you know it was coming especially to get you.  —ali-*

Black women are more apt than black men to be hoodwinked by the more subtle forms of oppression in that sometimes the loss of a privilege is not directly related to an abuse of that privilege. Ordinarily, the loss or denial of a promotion should be work-related, but many times can be class-related (making way for a white person), and  the sista blames herself.  By identifying with  the loss (or sense thereof), she does not focus on the fact that it is not tied to her performance in any significant way, but rather  is related directly to her as a black woman. It is imply another instance or race and gender aiding and betting workplace racism. Sistas must give careful consideration to the fact  that any issue that could effect  significant changes in her future behavior may not, at all, be performance-related, but is, as brothas know, a more subtle form of oppression that can  grab you when you least expect it.

## November 19

*A phony smile is simply the opening act of a prelude to betrayal.  –ali–*

Here's some food for thought.  Sistas  have been lulled into complacency due to the fact of their high profile visibility in politics and the corporate world. There's a reason for this visibility. *Visibility makes you a better target*!.. Ponder this  sistas.  How can white America approve of you when you produce, invent, and give birth to the most despised individual on the planet---the black man!!!?. Shouldn't common sense dictate that the same disdain visited upon the product will also be reserved for the producer.  Don't be fooled by the smiles and the pats on the back.   They are merely an elaborate floor show for betrayal.

November 20

*Poverty is the raw material of hunger.     –ali-*

Another stop on the journey for the black woman is not to compromise her inner drive to personally excel by not looking for opportunities to conduct herself as a business professional. Do not be afraid to focus on  individual success and don't be shy about entertaining objectives that extend beyond the home.   That's not selfish.   That's self-interest, a cornerstone to the preservation of the self.   Your self-interests are what permits you to become the architect of your future as they are the primary building blocks within your blueprint for success. Among other things, such as drive, desire, and determination, they will distinguish whether you have developed an outline for positive action or a flat-line for failure.  While you may never be able to figure out exactly what to expect if you are successful, you should never experience any doubts as to the expectations of not trying.  It's basically failure without the technical support of attempting to stand on your own 2 feet.

# November 21

*The 2$^{nd}$ line of defense for the sista is to be good and damn sure that her 1$^{st}$ line of defense is not relying on a man to take care of her.   –ali-*

The second line of defense for the black woman in the war not to become an invisible, disposable component of her man's impotence will be to intensify her efforts to be optimistic.  This means coordinating exact strategies to lower barriers and eliminate biases against you because this will signal the determination of your impending independence to the world.  Clear policy is forever the turning point in closing out and dismantling the failure of your prior actions, but even then you cannot be slow to grasp the nature of your problem.  You are in default specifically because you are the derivative of this country's not knowing what to do with the black man.  You must stand up.  You possess no hedge.  You have nothing to swap.  And even though you were swept into this mess by your exposure to us (black men), you will be contained with the same restraints.  Now consider this.  Your presence in the workplace is not needed in  great numbers, and in no sphere of economic activity do you exercise either control or influence.  This means you are a liability.  Guess what happens next?  *You're next!*  Once the disposal of the black man is complete, it's your turn. Better check it out, girl.

## November 22

*Death is not a passing grade in the School Of Hard Knocks. Survival is.   —ali-*

A birth certificate is your diploma from the womb.   That is your first victory. Build on it. Expand. Grow.   You must live as though you intend to master the complexities of life. You started out with a passing grade. You survived 9 months of being lost and alone, so now it's time to live out loud.   To be invisible is not a claim to fame, so if you're "aiming to be famous", you gotta let life know you're here.

## November 23

*In a war, you must never seek equality with your enemy. It is superiority that you desire. –ali-*

You, black woman, can always decipher something about how much you are hated when you line up your vital interests side-by-side with the interests of those in control. If you do not weigh in on the strong side of the balance of power, then you must invent another apparatus to resolve your helplessness. Your struggle is less about being sized up for equality as it is over future stabilization. And for that to occur by any significant measure, *the black man must remain intact!* This demands that you simultaneously employ your traditional strength to upholding the black man while at the same time holding back the white man. Why soft-pedal the problem? You do not possess the luxury to pick over the wreckage, or to choose a one-sided plan of action. Sitting still, standing mute, and waiting on deliverance has contrived to rob you of these options. We are in big trouble, so don't hesitate. Put the pedal to the metal! Go fast! Come quick! Get here!

## November 24

*Celebrate ... ...Rejoice .....Sing.....Shout ... ...Roar*
Celebrate.....You should incorporate as much fanfare as possible into your **_"coming-out-of-the=darkness"_** party. Have a gift-giving ceremony for yourself. Rejoice..... Decorate your new existence by anointing yourself with a new name. Sing..... You are the latest newcomer to the community of the aware, and it's vital that your arrival be noted and announced., so make it authentic and real. Your very $1^{st}$ contribution to yourself and others is that everyone knows you are here. Shout..... Affirm the moment by embedding it in the memorable affairs of the universe. Embellish it with the involvement of all your significant others, so they may honor your rebirth. Roar

## November 25

*Who goes there is sometimes not as important as
what goes where?   -ali-*

Never toy with the love of your boyfriend
And don't ever forget his due
Don't ever feel free to overprotect your son
Although both may  be your "Boo".
Just because your mother gave you birth
She has no right to run your life
You still can be a woman and daddy's lil' girl
And not fall into strife.
There's never a need to ignore your friends
With your loyalty, you can always be fair
As long as you make it a point of knowing
The importance of what goes where.

## November 26

*The shorter the hem of a woman's skirt is a direct reflection of the strength of her man's morals.* —
*ali-*

The black woman in America has always been an open door into the agonized soul of the black man. Whenever the white man has sought a personalized audience with the black man in absentia, all he has ever had to do was to peek in on the sistas. That's why peddlers, salesmen, cops always ask to speak to the woman of the house. They know that an "unknowing" sista can be turned into a trusted spy on the state of her nigga

November 27

*The pillow is always  softest when you're laying
your head where it shouldn't  be.  —ali-*

This is a **Sista Alert!**  There is no established time-frame where it will ever become permissible for circumstance or condition to wake you up and make you wise.  This is a no-no that would disrupt the nature of your dependency and hopelessness. The length of your stay at the threshold of unproductiveness is held to be the time it takes you to learn that procrastination is a curse. Help yourself. NOW!!!

## November 28

*Oh yes, he does the windows too! (the saga of the window-dresser)*

Dig this! Tokenism is the professional equivalent of sleeping with someone else's husband, so beware of it. It is a phenomena that preys on gullible people since the subtle complexities of tokenism can bear so many similarities to your own individual achievements that it can be difficult to put your finger on just what you've truly accomplished and what you actually take credit for. In addition, tokenism performs its song-and-dance routine so well that you are easily influenced to overlook the fact that you're stealing from your personal growth by excelling at becoming a professional window-dresser. In retrospect, tokenism has been historically reserved for those individuals who are hard-working, high-achievers who think that freedom means "FREE-TO-DO-ME". Dig that

## November 29

*Don't give a toast to the fool. Toast the fool.*   *–ali-*
America is no safe place for fools. You can look at the numbers and clearly see that they are either dead or in jail, or waiting for one or the other to happen to them. There is no such place as a fool's paradise, so don't search for it. You must become more conscious of the fact that fools do abound in society and that their unproductivity is a burden you don't want to share, so concentrate on making a fool out those who wish to make you a fool. Let's put an end to foolishness.

■■■■■■■■■■■■■■■■■■■■■■■■■■■■■■■■■■■■■■■■■■■

November 30

Once more. THIS IS AMERICA AND THERE ARE THOSE WHO ARE VEHEMENTLY OPPOSED TO YOU GETTING AHEAD!

# December 1

*Sadness or euphoria always depend on how deeply you are  committed to what you choose to do about tomorrow....-ali-*

When.....If.....As you embark on the rewarding and remarkable journey too YOU, you must heed the time-honored discipline of  truth. As a consequence, you will not be able to escape the reality that from time to time you have made significant contributions to your own destruction.  These errors against yourself probably did nothing to improve the overall quality of you life, and to be honest, more than likely they only influenced you to complement your adverse situation with the willingness to adjust to it.  Your life is a measurement, and the days thereof are the critical and vital resources which you invest to either extend or suspend happiness.  In order to make a fair estimate of your future, you must learn how to evaluate every decision you make because they communicate the depths of your commitment to yourself.  You should note that decisions are the "language of life" and it is these that will expose you to either sadness or euphoria, so it is crucial to understand how (relevant) information is a necessary instrument of decision-making. It (relevant info) protects you from irresponsibility or the need for a crystal ball. Tomorrows are always more promising when you have decided upon their content. Decide now to make a happy place for yourself in tomorrow.

# December 2

*An opinion about you is in 'name only', but your
opinion of yourself is the law.   –ali-*

Of all the many things that are influential in establishing   (and generally maintaining) your 'squatters' right' (the state of being where you choose to exist) none is more important than your ability to identify for yourself your role in what happens to and becomes of you!. As the sole owner of the highest opinion about you, you can only disrupt the continuity of this opinion once you entertain the assumption that it is in your best interests to become a resource rather than a source. (Note the essential difference)  As a source, you become a liability to yourself because your relevancy is limited to a specific moment in time. As a resource, your influence remains current throughout all periods of time.  Hence, the main prerequisite of clearly establishing the identity of your role is to understand that an opinion about you is in *name only,* but that your opinion of yourself s the real driving force behind how far you will go for yourself. One word of caution, though. When you are well-versed in the high opinion of yourself, forever is as far as you can go!

## December 3

*Ignorance is nature's warning sticker that cautions
you to avoid men who are foolish.   –ali–*

Did you know that each day comes with a set of instructions. In practice, we are instructed to give thanks and praises to The Creator  for the grant and privilege of a new moment.   In theory, we are instructed to match our efforts with whatever we accomplished on yesterday and to improve ourselves since it is theoretically unacceptable to attempt to earn results from a moment whose time has passed. Yesterday is  disbursed into eternity and the ensuing changes should trigger a constant re-adjustment in our perspective or else we stagnate, becoming  rooted in a time sequence that only approximates the reality of what actually and truly is. This standing still or perpetual "dragging-of-the-feet" accounts for many of the "near misses' and most of the "came close" that have a dual purpose in life.  (1) They instruct us that no matter how good, great, or successful yesterday  may have been, once it is past, any yielded information about it is inaccurate, incomplete and misleading as regards the accountability of today. Change has taken place and since change specifically effects everything required to make timely decisions, proper adjustments must be made. (2) They instruct us to follow instructions.

## December 4

*Every sale in the marketplace of life will either*
*uplift o diminish your reputation.  –ali–*

You are a biz'ness.  As such, you must have
supplies on hand if you intend to be a success, In
the competitive biz'ness of selling yourself to the
world, included among your supplies are your
ethics.  These determine your duty towards doing
right or wrong. Neither is a prepaid commodity
although your conscience is held in pledge for their
use or abuse.  No one can guarantee your reputation
but you, and your reputation is a reaction to how
easy or difficult it is for money to obsess and/or
possess you.

## December 5

*Black folks may never learn how to add up the numbers but they damn sho' know how to add up the facts.  –ali-*

Your mind is a depreciable asset and it reaches the end of its estimated usefulness once you opt to become enslaved.  Your mind is no longer a precision instrument  once you dull it by non-use. Even while there may never be any exact measurement on the damage inflicted upon one human by letting another human think and choose for him, it is nonetheless a devastating blow against an individual's service to self. During the entire course of this travesty, your internal privilege to function meaningfully is interrupted and exchanged for the external evidence of your subservience.  In essence, you have cleared the 1$^{st}$  hurdle to becoming a poster-child of the equation that states:Your brawn *plus* someone else's  brain *multiplied* by another's bankroll *divides*  your ass into a *subtraction* of a man!

## December 6

*Due to you depends on what you do for you...-ali-*

Meanwhile....under no circumstances can you bank on hope because a wing and a prayer are not pertinent means of producing results. Remember that.   Also remember this.  The common, current mode of production for rewarding results are "flying under the drift of your own hard efforts". Having (or compelling) others to do for you must be viewed for what it is.  No matter how much they pretend, no one in their right frame of mind is an overly enthusiastic learner when introduced  to info and/or situations that will strictly benefit you. Don't forget that altruism in much of this world is very unfamiliar terrain.  DO 4 U.

## December 7

*Don't wreck-----spot check...-ali-*

Don't neglect to spot check yourself. Never underestimate the power of estimation. This prevents avoidable and unjustifiable judgment errors as well as precludes you from devaluing any of your strengths. It is a mental relationship that puts and keeps both your strengths and weakness in prospective. This spot-check is especially warranted before you approve yourself worthy of making any binding decisions of the moment. In all situations, cost and loss must be calculated because they are the features that determine winners and losers, so don't wreck...Spot-check.

## December 8

*Looking at yourself is the best way to see. –ali-*

Over time, spot checks must give way to a full-blown personal assessment. Nothing but this will allow an accurate inventory of who you are, and where you will be able to go based on what you are working with. And it all emerges from a detailed description of where you feel you ought to be in life, and where you actually are. The unabridged distance between the 2 is the specific identification of your skills not matching up to the value of your goals. This denotes weakness and any weakness that is dehabilitating hints at your need for greater control over either the perceptions of your strengths or the manner by which you exercise them. What must immediately occur now is an internal reconciliation where any weaknesses (doubt, fear, hopelessness etc) must be collapsed and every strength vouched for. As a normal consequence of bad judgment, you simply define your losses, age your goals, and give yourself credit for initiating changes to reflect the changed conditions of the playing field.

December 9

*Luck ain't nuthin' but the withheld social security
benefits of a job well done   –ali–*

Don't even think about it. Luck merely compensates for inaccurate actions giving you a false sense of hope in your window of opportunity. In theory, luck is the residue of gains that you failed to properly assess. Viewed thusly, luck is simply the trademark of an intangible exchange that was not recognized at an earlier date, and is nothing more that market value for your sweat, so appreciate it if it comes to you but do not attempt to raise it to life on your own.

December 10

*Willpower is the exclusive power of your mind*
*beating the hell out of discouragement. –ali–*

Check out this science. Willpower is a natural resource that you must never abandon even when you feel it is exhausted because the physical life of your willpower exists in full force until you are dead! It weakens or will weaken only in response to how much you limit, surrender, or retire it. *Willpower is the exclusive privilege of mind exceeding and surpassing discouragement.* It is the goodwill ambassador of your soul and articulates to the world that in any enterprise you undertake that you will be reckoned with. Willpower is one of the most distinctive features of your psyche. It has the technical characteristics of a drill sergeant and the recognized potential of a king.

## December 11

*The only way to make heads or tail out of your existence is never to head in on the tail end of your potential. –ali–*

Make heads of this. The most logical explanation for failure is that it is an unknown, unseen risk until a loss occurs. Never is it a permanent stigma affixed to anyone's life that assigns or reduces that life to significant adversity. So the question is do you make the prediction that doing nothing will minimize both risk and loss or do you participate in your existence? Of course, you act. Then you do what comes next. ANALYZE. Now you can make choices instead of predictions, and that is a giant bunny hop. You know why? Because everyone's life evolves around a certain trend, that's why. If the trend in your family is to be Muslim, then chances are, so will you. Whether the trend of your environment produces lawyers, doctors, pimps, or prostitutes, then there is a good chance you'll fall into the respective groove. This is also known by what I call *"comparative living"*. This is your ability to analyze the trend, in whole or in part, and focus on the effect it has had on others and then compare this relationship to your situation. Does it enhance or inhibit your future goals? If the trend indicators are positives to you, then you're in the house, but what if not? You run because running away provides you a minimum basis for future success

## December 12

*Success demands that you never stop growing. –*
*ali-*

Isn't it funny that even in the performance of your duty to yourself, your activity level will be decided by the volume of your fear to be successful. Ain't that something? It's as though some people don't actually desire success. Instead, they enjoy living between the opportunities produced by success. Theirs is a sort of pre-determined existence where they pour forth all their energy to remain in a self-imposed controlled economic environment. They strive for the traditional standard between the rise and fall of their convenient mediocrity, so don't be fooled by the monetary gains they sometimes accrue. It is simply vacation pay and won' begin to increase substantially until they go to work full time at being a real success. Don't attempt to adjust the headphones. Change your tune.

## December 13

*The best way to keep from getting lost is to know where you're going before you get there.* —ali-

**Super**. Or **Stupor**.. Those are the cubbyholes where your life will fit. Choose one or the other. Choose carefully. It should come as no surprise that getting stuck in "stupor" is not so cute, and that it is excruciatingly difficult to get a boost up and/or out of that fix. As a matter of fact, there is no quick fix or common cure. Basically, you're the heir to a nightmare. Your world now is a satellite image of elaborate special effects designed to make you feel as if you are nothing more to the universe than a job cut on the payroll of life; an aerodynamic zero. You are substantially less than a penny saved…. By now, you should get the message, so think constantly of how easy it is to make mistakes with your existence. Each individual must make his/her own push for quality and to establish a life hat does not rest on rigged-up out-of-date props. Just be you. You will learn to like it once you realize that your name can be brand name. You are a winner. All that you have to do is step through the portal. You are now leaving Stupor…..

## December 14

*A  TV  is the only set of boobs that don't provide
milk. It  milks you.  –ali-*

Television may suggest improvements in the
content of your life, but not its context.  It may also
seek to help you look or feel better, but never how
to live better.  Why?  Because TV can only provide
advice for those whose primary motivation is to
consume a second opinion that there-is-not-enough-
to-go-around-so-you-better-get-it-while-it-lasts, and
for this reason, TV should be intended primarily for
internal use (entertainment) and  at  no time for an
external accounting of your affairs.  A good rule of
thumb is this:  You own your TV, it does not own
you.  Whenever you permit the  TV to audit your
household, growing emphasis will be placed on
your need to be gainfully employed by your desires

## December 15

*Birth is a simple acknowledgment that evolves into a growing pronouncement to live only after you proclaim your profound declaration to exist.*  *—ali-*

There are great expectations that exist regarding a life worth living or fighting for. 1st, you either must enjoy what you represent or you must like what you can become. Otherwise, you cannot benefit from being exposed to the best within you because it will be impossible for you to recognize you own individual worth and potential. In such a state, the most you can do is to borrow from your self-esteem and promise to pay back later. But you never do. STOP! Get on the good foot! You are traveling on the left-handed side of your soul, but it is not too late. By your ignorance of self, you have merely placed an order for failure. Cancel it. There is a procedure for this. It's called "riding the gravy train". Here's how it works. Start with a ***simple acknowledgment*** of your right-to-be and then allow this to spill over into a ***growing pronouncement*** of your right-to-be which will open up into a ***profound declaration*** of your right-to-be. Now, that's making gravy, baby. Right On!

# December 16

*A birth certificate is your diploma from the womb.*
*Successful people graduate summa cum laude.  –*
*ali-*

A major requirement of successful living is that it be understood that each day is so much more than a mere 24 hour period.  It is a personal chronological display of how well you have handled or mastered whatever-came-next.  Frequently, you may be compelled to check, cross-reference or chase down the origin of your success to some ardent student, fan, or admirer, but  being truly self-evolved, you will have the advantage of knowing exactly  from whence it started.  Simply point to you birth certificate and say: "I WAS BORN TO BE SUCCESSFUL". The truth  could never sound sweeter.

December 17

*A bad habit is a mistake waiting to happen.  –Ali-*

**Shit happens!**    Mistakes are commonly recognized as the general expenses of living, irregardless of how they are performed.  Similarly, bad habits are the company they (mistakes) keep, and bad habits are easy converts, especially when under the pressure of not knowing their asses from their elbow. Just consider that the graduation rate of a bad habit is zero if you exercise care and caution in your affairs, and magna cum laude if you go public with your stupidity!  Beware.  One of the most visible characteristics of a bad habit is its ability to follow instructions from a fool and then execute them like a rocket scientist.  You also must remember that you can challenge a bad habit, but you must live with the consequences of a mistake. Shit happens, but that is not as bad as what happens to shit when a bad habit gets a degree.

## December 18

*To be invisible is not a claim to fame, so if you're*
*"aiming to be famous" you gotta let life see ya.*
*–ali–*

It's a personal thang. Only you can determine the optimum size of how large you want to live. Generally, it is the limit self-imposed upon you by your reaction and response to the universal question of "*what if?*  Most people of color relate to "what if" as though it is some package deal consolidated with "everything-that-can-go-wrong-in-their-lives". *What if I don't get the job?....What if he/she doesn't like me?.....What if I don't know what to do?....* As long as you fear the big "What if" dilemma, you will function in a controlled environment that demands compliance and conformity where everyone is in cohoots to reach the same goal: invisibility. Everyone in that environment is assigned the same duty: to be competent at *just-getting-by*. Do not allow "What If" to become your custodian. It is nothing more than a 'round-about way to meet, greet, and beat yourself over the head.

December 19

*Minus family----You lack everything....-ali-*

Before you panic, remember these tips.
1) Life is always precious.
2) Don't trust the government.
3) The check is not in the mail.
4) Sometimes, you must break the rules.
5) You cannot get even with life.
6) Life made you a child. You must make yourself a man.
7) There is always time to do something constructive.
8) A fertile imagination is the playground of success.
9) To get a grip, you must 1$^{st}$ extend your hand.
10) The most prized gift is family.

# December 20

*Fight fire with fire and never give up. You never know what God has in store for you. —ali—*

Who do you think you are? How dare you reverse the fundamental criteria of life by quitting? It just may be that destiny has you on hold, awaiting your moment. It just may be that the events of your existence have been conditioning you, readying you for startling, eye-opening success. The quitter never knows what tomorrow would have unraveled in the path of his journey, and no matter how difficult times are, no living being possesses the genuine persona to up and cease to perform as his own greatest advocate. On the path of life's journey, there is no trajectory for this dizzying loop into dissolution, and this failure-on-impact was not meant to be, so don't inspect or consider this monumental aberration. It is a misrepresentation of your responsibility and obligation to directly indulge in all of the good things that God has placed on the earth. There is no real need for you to stumble towards the truth. It stares you in the face. You are worthy, and the worthy always work well when working well is worth working for.

## December 21

*If you know where you want to go, then you should also know how long the train has been gone and when it is coming back.* –ali–

Life is an one-of-a-kind item and people, in general, will opt for the method of examination that best suits or fits their personal conditions. Historically, African-Americans have settled for either the GOWG (Going Out With Glory)style or the "Lord-my-feet-sho'-are-tired" method. Both are magnets for manipulation where the end results differ only in the substance and form of the pain brought on by their use. Both support the acknowledgment that you are either superior or inferior to the assumption that there is a pre-arranged maximum or minimum amount of "stuff" needed to gain contentment. However, in reality, your "stuff" quotient will neither qualify nor disqualify you from suffering. Thus neither mode of living is expressive of a life well-lived. GOWG expresses brevity and excess while the other calls forth longevity and impoverishment. Between the pair are many other roads, any of which can lead to successful living. You must choose. With knowledge of self (and your goals) choose. If you know where you want to go, then you should also know the road to take to get there. People, get ready.

# December 22

*Don't be concerned so with the overhead cost of living that you pay little attention to the Over-The-Head-Boss-Of-Giving.*   *–ali–*

For as long as you breathe, you are a work-in-progress no matter at what stage of development. You would be wise to note that it is death that is the "finished goods" of life and not your personal achievements, so slow down. Enjoy what has been assigned to you by way of your own strivings. Understand that all our individual activities, good or bad, tied end-to-end are, spiritually speaking, nothing more than untraceable labor as far as death is concerned. What this illustrates is that despite all the recent innovations and all the stress from trying to keep up with the Jones, there is a definite need to relax. To do this rightly, you must never get pushed out of your spiritual corner. Become a part-time busybody for your own rest and relaxation, but don't get lazy. And keep in mind that your actions are documentation that will yield 2 different reports; one for man to base his eulogy; the other for God to make His judgment. PRAY!!! In the spiritual world, there is no breaking even......

## December 23

*It's not so much the double standard of society that worries me. It's the double punishment.  —ali-*

Black folks in this country must always remember to adjust their sights to cover the passive racism of so-called justice.  A white woman who sits at home on her ass all day long is regarded as a full-time homemaker. A sista who does the same is called unemployed. This difference raises a question about the integrity of those who call the shots and it also clarifies that justice still means "just us' in this country.  We must lean on the fact that the amount of justice we receive in this country does not in any way depend upon what we are actually due. It is more closely related to the current value of the white man's  private fears about us. In Amerikkka, the scales of justice are not tilted by the weighing-in of right and wrong.  Instead, it balances itself under the direct pressure of the white man's guilt upon himself. When  the pressure dips too much, then he will donate some justice, but even then it will be done as a charitable contribution and never as a matter of right.  And that's still wrong. So if you ever decide to seek justice, know that she is not only blind, but that the bitch is also deaf, dumb, crippled and crazy.  Just so you'd know.

# December 24

*A coincidence is a 1<sup>st</sup> round draft choice of all hell-getting-ready-to-break-loose.* —ali

Get this through your head. To be successful at anything you attempt, you should never mistake coincidence for a pattern. Be real. If there exists a pattern of clearly ineffectual, dead-end planning or operating blunders in your scheme of things, why risk thinking they are mere coincidences. Get this. Coincidence is a side-show staged by circumstances outside of your control. A clear pattern (of errors) is your brain functioning at its highest level of incompetency. Also note that a coincidence becomes a rival to the security of your aspirations only when you ignore its vitality. It will grow more provocative and once it is drafted into a pattern, the harder it will be to blow its cover. And this is the most powerful reason to bait your trap well. Coincidences are lurking, ready to confuse you. They are proof that in your quest for success, there will be "eyes" and "ears" everywhere, and in their characteristic "pop-out-of-nowhere- fashion will take every opportunity to spook you, so don't let them make it out of boot camp. If by now, you haven't glimpsed the enemy, secretly and carefully glance into the mirror. Get the picture!

## December 25

Compromise doesn't mean selling out
And being patient shouldn't imply waiting forever
Playing it safe does not mean being risk-free
And the future is no place near never.
Your day in the sun shouldn't suggest going-to-hell
And welfare is not "getting paid
An act of faith does not hush you up
Or condemn you to the bed you just made
Nigga is not  term of endearment
And a sista is never a bitch
Sex cannot be a stand-in for love
Any more that a hole can be called a ditch.
Words are the makers or breakers of soul
They are the magic that governs you
So not only be mindful of the words you speak
Be careful of what they make you do

## December 26

*Current events are the  shallow waters of life.*
*History is the ocean.   –ali–*

Never ignore your debt to your  heritage. When calculating what you owe, just remember that you are who you are based on who your ancestors were, and that the relationship between us and them should never be broken.  Strengthen these ties by observing, celebrating, and/or commemorating the legacies they have bequeathed to us. You must absorb yourself, immerse yourself in our history. This is no subsidiary occurrence.  It is our direct support system, so love it,  live it, and never leave it. Give Kwanza its due; make Juneteenth sparkle and grow.  Observe Malcolm's birthday (May 19th) as well as Dr. King's. Be Afrocentric in February, but most of all-------pay homage to yourself. Loving yourself is always a great moment in African-American History.

# December 27

*As for suggestions, carefully check out their warranty. It may be that the one you're borrowing has already been used one time too many. —ali—*

Keep this in mind. On your journey to self and success, it is **_answers_** you want, not suggestions. While suggestions may sometimes evolve into 'news you can use', borrowing from someone else's experience can be very risky. Suggestions, by their very nature, are fragile and given the fact that their development evolved from outside your personal experiences, they can mislead. Don't forget that a suggestion is nothing more than a one-quarter solution to your problem. It is merely proof that something did work for someone else. It may or it <u>may not</u> work for you. Therefore seek **ANSWERS**! The truth is that life is a very active process and to rely upon suggestions as a reference is to court disaster. <u>**SEEK ANSWERS!**</u>. They are the ageless weather vanes of life that clearly inform you of which way the wind blows. To insulate yourself from disappointment, invest in answers. Your capacity to survive depends upon them, so no matter how tantalizing a suggestion may be, just remember that even at its deepest level, it is simply a testimonial to your trust in someone other than yourself.

## December 28

*When you know where all the bones are buried, you can stomp wit' the big dawgs. –ali–*

There will never be a death knell for failure and the bells will never toll for those who will take advantage of you. So what does this means? It means you must compete. It implies that you must challenge yourself to arrive at correct and viable solutions. It means that you must regulate. Since there are no rules either in the jungle or at the bottom of the heap, you $1^{st}$ step to getting on track is to get to a level of existence where there is understandable order. You can always compete more effectively when everyone is protected or constrained by the same rules. Dig this. By *recognizing the rules,* you can better organize your options and choices. By *remembering the rules*, you can act upon them wisely and introduce timely innovations that may allow you a slight advantage. By *living the rules,* you can put yourself in a position to make them! In essence, you rule only when you know the rules.

## December 29

*If you want to fit in, you better fix it  - ali-*

Now is the time to dialogue with yourself and to carve out any necessary fundamental  shifts in your focus because there will be no Mr.  Fix-It around the corner waiting to fit-you-in.  Getting left at the bus stop is the ultimate scandal which means you have been caught with your drawers(or panties) down. And for this, there is no gift certificate. Without a doubt, the moment of now is always your most pivotal time to change.  Do It!  Dramatically unleash yourself.  Release yourself.   You are the epitome of everything needed to be a winner in the race of life.  Nothing or no one can stop you but you, so get out  of the way of yourself.  You're a train coming through and you can't be slowed down, so don't be concerned about how fast you go. There   will   always   be   plenty   of   track. **Choo…..Choo…..Choo…..**

## December 30

*When you don't know who you are, it's hard to
convince others that you're not a fool.   –ali–*

Wanna hear something funny?  Ever since day 1
in this country, some black folks have suffered from
what I call the  **"recognition condition"**.  This
means they do not recognize who they are and
voluntarily opt to pretend to be something else. At
the turn of the century, the accepted pretense was to
*pass for white*. Unfortunately (or fortunately) the
charge for  "passing" was a very light complexion
which excluded many blacks.  However, during this
century, this limiting restriction (light skin) was
systemically replaced with a new, non-exclusive
condition.  It's called  **"jumping-the-tracks-and-
never-coming-back".**  Now, even blacker-than-the-
Ace-of-spades brothas and sistas could effectively
pass for white.  How?  By depriving the black
community access to their knowledge and expertise.
How much whiter can you can?  This has been the
black man's scourge.  CHECK THIS OUT.
Whenever an enemy wishes to destroy an enemy,
they 1$^{st}$ destroy all the learned ones for without a
doubt, a people without knowledge will perish.
When successful people of color forget their roots
and withhold their assistance from those left in the
hood, then the combined magnitude of their
**"recognition condition"** is terminal for everybody.
And that ain't no joke.

## December 31

*Any time your life is consumed by the flames of ignorance, the degree of the burn depends on how* long *it takes you to realize that no one can put out the fire but you.* –ali-

Failure is legendary in that it has overcome all efforts to contain, control, or eradicate it, so do not mistake, underestimate or overlook this fact. Only the dead and the unborn are exempt from it. Everyone else is fair prey. And in case you've forgotten what failure is, I'll remind you. Failure is the eyes-wide-open disposal of your common sense! And good ol' common sense is the same conceptual framework that never allows us to forget that fire burns. That's the logic behind common sense. It never attempts to replace what you already know. Instead, it re-emphasizes that knowledge. That's why our reaction to fire is always the same which means you have mastered the basic fundamentals of common sense. Now, all you have to do is to apply this principle to managing and off-setting failure. **WAKE UP! WAKE UP! YOUR LIFE IS ON FIRE!**

**WAKE UP> WAKE UP> YOUR LIFE IS ON FIRE.**

www.ingramcontent.com/pod-product-compliance
Lightning Source LLC
Chambersburg PA
CBHW051813090426
42736CB00011B/1456